Ghanaian Cook Book

Favourite Recipes
from Ghana

Sophia Manu (Ed)

©2006 Adaex Educational Publications Ltd

All rights reserved.
No part of this publication may be reproduced, stored, in a retrieval system or transmitted in any form or by any means without prior permission from the publishers.

ISBN: 9988-573-61-8

2R McCarthy Hill
Accra, Ghana West Africa

Editor: Sophia Manu

Editorial Advisor: S. Asare Konadu

Cover design and typesetting: Kwadwo Osei-Safo

May 2010

Dear Lisa,

I thought of you when I saw this book. Maybe you should collect cookbooks from around the world?

Love so much,
Gigi

Content

1.	Baked Foods	7
2.	Fried Foods	33
3.	Roasted Foods	51
4.	Steamed Foods	62
5.	Boiled Foods	73
6.	Soups	98
7.	Stewed Foods	112
8.	Vegetables	135
9.	Sweets	144
10.	Miscellenous	169
11.	Index	171

Introduction

Boys and girls love mixing ingredients. They are at an age before cooking becomes the chore of continuous meal making and they find the whole experience exciting.

This book has been designed to serve all sections of people, from the casual visitor to Ghana who wants to taste truly Ghanaian dish, the busy mother in a family, to domestic science students in schools and other institutions and the woman with a home and a job.

Much as we take delight in cooking for
(a) The sake of cooking
(b) Cooking to illustrate a project
(c) Cooking to prove an experiment
(d) Cooking for the family,

We should take note of hygiene, safety into consideration.

Too many cases of food poisoning occur and everyone should be cautious in handling anything to do with food — Ingredients, cloths and utensils with care.

Hands must be washed before starting to cook. Tasting spoon should be washed before returning it to the mixture. Washing-up utensils particularly is important and should be left dry before packing them to avoid mould and rust.

Bins for food waste should be covered and place yards away from clean food.

Cooking in any place involves potentially dangerous equipments and safety measures would have to be observed.

For example, do not wipe over an electric cooker until the main switch has been put off.

Kitchen knives should be handled carefully to avoid injury.

With these in mind, cooking would then be an exciting pastime, routine etc.

It is my hope that this book will bring variety and new pleasures to your table.

Weights and Measures

Until recently when a vigorous campaign has been set up to encourage the use of scales, measurements have always been in homely weights which have long been the standard of measurements in most homes, vocational schools and restaurants etc.

Where a scale is available as shown, it would be appropriate and accurate to use it as a measurer.

However, below are the homely weights and measures for various ingredients.

Light Ingredients

Flour, Cornflour, Custard Powder, Bread-Crumps, Grated Coconut

1	Heaped tablespoon	approx. ...	1oz.
1	Heaped dessertspoon	approx. ...	$1/2$ oz.
1	Heaped tablespoon	approx. ...	$1/4$ oz.
2	Heaped tablespoon bread-crumbs	approx. ...	1oz.
$1^1/_2$	Heaped tablespoon grated coconut	approx. ...	1oz.
1	cig. tin flour	approx. ...	$1/4$ lb.

Heavy Ingredients

Sugar, Rice, Groundnuts, Beans

1	Cig. tin rice	approx. ...	$1/2$ lb.
1	Cig. tin groundnuts	approx. ...	$1/2$ lb.
1	Cig. tin beans	approx. ...	$1/2$ lb.
4	Cubes sugar	approx. ...	1oz.
1	Tablespoon butter or lard	approx. ...	1oz.

Liquids

1	Beer bottle	...	4 cups or approx. $1^{1}/_{4}$ pts.
1	Gill	...	1 cup or approx. $^{1}/_{4}$ pt.
2	Cups	...	... approx. $^{1}/_{2}$ pt.

Baked Foods

1. Fam

4 well ripe plantain	Onions,	salt
1 pt. palm oil	pepper	
½ lb. ground corn or dough		

Peel and beat the plantain until free from lumps. Mix it with the ground corn, pepper, onions and salt. Add the palm oil. Cut into shapes and bake in a hot oven for 30 minutes. Serve either hot or cold.

2. Apiti

10 very ripe plantains	1 lb. dough
Salt	Plantain leaves

Pound the plantain until free from lumps. Add the dough and a little salt and mix well. Divide it into pieces and wrap each in a dry plantain. Bake in a hot oven for 30 minutes. Serve with roasted groundnuts.

3. Garri Biscuits

5 cassava	3 eggs	6 ozs. sugar
Nutmeg	Milk	A little flour

Peel the cassava, clean and grate them. Beat the eggs and milk together. Add in the grated cassava. Add sugar and the grated nutmeg. Sieve in a little flour, mix well. Roll out and cut into shapes and bake for about 15 minutes.

4. Coconut Buns

1 lb flour	8 ozs. sugar

6 ozs. butter or margarine	
4 eggs	Milk
2 teasp. baking powder	4 ozs. grated coconut

Cream the butter and the sugar. Beat the eggs and add a little milk to them. Sieve the dry ingredients into a basin. Add to the creamed butter and sugar the liquid and flour by degrees, making a very stiff dough. Place in small rough heaps on a greased baking tin and bake in a hot oven for about 20 minutes.

5. Rich Banana Cake

3 ripe bananas	10 ozs. flour
4 ozs. butter	5 ozs. castor sugar
1 gill milk	2 teasp. baking powder
Vanilla	A pinch of salt
4 eggs	

Cream the butter and the sugar. Add the prepared bananas. Add flour, beaten eggs and milk alternatively. Beat well between each addition. Pour into a greased cake tin and bake in a moderate oven for about 45 minutes.

6. Polo Biscuits

12 ozs. flour	8 ozs. baking sugar
6 eggs	2 coconuts
3 ozs. butter	$1/2$ pt. milk

Grate the coconuts. Separate the yolks of the eggs from the whites. Beat the yolks and add to the milk, add 6 ozs. sugar. Stir in the grated coconuts. Melt the butter and add to the mixture. Sieve in the flour gradually. Mix and turn on to a floured board and roll out to about $1/2$ inch in thickness. Beat the whites of the eggs to a froth and add the rest of sugar. Brush this lightly over the pastry and cut into shapes. Put on a greased tin and bake in a hot oven from 15 to 20 minutes.

7. Aberewa-Nnwe

1 lb. four	6 ozs. sugar
4 eggs	1 oz. butter or margarine
1 teasp. nutmeg	1 gill milk
1 teasp. baking powder	

Beat the eggs and the sugar together. Add the butter to the flour and baking powder. Add the beaten eggs. Add nutmeg and a little milk. Knead it and put it on a floured board. Roll it to the required thickness and cut into fancy shapes. Sprinkle flour over them and bake in a moderate oven till brown (about 20 minutes).

8. Corn Cake

Corn dough	Salt	Plantain	Sugar

Pound the plantain and mix with the dough. Add sugar and a pinch of salt. Roll into small balls, wrap in leaves and bake in a moderate oven for half an hour.

9. Grilled Fish and Pineapple

A plate of cassava chips, 3 herrings or fresh haddock steaks, 2 pine-apple rings, cut into chunks, 1 oz. butter, salt and pepper.

Empty the cassava chips into the bottom of a serving dish and place to warm. Arrange the fish and drained pineapple chunks on grill rack. Dot fish with butter, sprinkle with salt and pepper. Place in oven and cook for 10–15 minutes turning once during cooking. Arrange fish steaks on top of crisps. Decorate with grilled pineapple chunks.

10. Little Iced Orange Buns

$1/4$ lb. margarine, $1/2$ lb. caster sugar,
1 large egg, 6 oz. self-raising flour, grated rind,
1 orange, 3 tablespoon strained orange juice.
Topping: 3 oz. sieved icing sugar, approx.
2 dessertspoons hot water,
orange slices cut in triangles to decorate.

Cream the margarine with the sugar until light and fluffy. Gradually beat in the egg. Fold in sieved flour, orange rind and juice. Grease bun tins and two-thirds fill with the mixture. Bake in a moderately hot oven 15–20 minutes until golden brown. Cool on a wire tray and add the topping.

To make topping: Mix the icing sugar with enough water to make a thick creamy consistency, and spread over each bun. Top each with a teaspoon of glace icing and a triangle of orange slice.

11. Chocolate Cream

> 6 ozs. butter or margarine, 6 ozs. caster sugar, 3 eggs, 5 ozs. self-raising flour, 1 ozs. cocoa powder, pinch of salt, approx. 1 teaspoon warm water. Butter Icing and decoration: $1/2$ lb. icing sugar, $1/4$ lb. butter or margarine, 3 level tablespoons cocoa powder, 1 tablespoon milk, few drops vanilla essence, rounded teaspoon instant coffee powder, 2 tablespoon hot water, 2–3 ozs. chocolate vermicelli, few chocolate buttons.

Grease and line base of two 8-inch sandwich tins. Cream butter or margarine and sugar together till light. Lightly whisk eggs and beat into creamed mixture. Fold in flour sifted with cocoa powder and salt. Add water to make dropping consistency. Divide mixture between prepared tins. Bake in moderately hot oven (390 deg. F. — Mark 5) for 25–30 minutes. Turn out, cool on wire rack. Remove paper. Sandwich cake round together with one third prepared butter icing. Spread a little over sides and top and roll in chocolate vermicelli. Place remainder in icing bag or tube fitted with star pipe and pipe edge with small scroll pattern. Repeat design in cake centre. Decorate with chocolate button sweets.

To make butter icing: Sift icing sugar and beat together with slightly softened butter or margarine until light and smooth. Beat in cocoa powder, milk, essence and instant coffee blended with hot water.

12. Pineapple Layer Cake

$1/4$ lb. butter or margarine, 5 ozs. caster sugar, 2 eggs, 7 ozs. self-raising flour, pinch salt, 1 ozs. ground rice, $1/4$ lb. canned pineapple, 1 tablespoon pineapple juice, pineapple pieces.

Filling: 2 ozs. butter or margarine, $1/4$ lb. sifted icing sugar, 1 dessertspoon warm milk, $1/4$ lb. canned pineapple.

Icing: $1/2$ lb. sifted icing sugar, squeeze lemon juice, a little pineapple juice, $1-1\frac{1}{2}$ tablelspoons warm water.

Grease and line 7-inch cake tin. Beat butter or margarine until soft, add sugar and beat until fluffy. Beat in eggs one at a time. Fold in flour sifted with salt and ground rice and add finely chopped and drained pineapple. Stir in the pineapple juice. Put mixture into the prepared tin. Bake in moderate oven (375 deg. F. — Mark 4) for 1 hour or until well risen and firm to the touch. Turn out and cool on wire rack. Halve cake and sandwich with cream filling. Coat cake with glace icing and decorate top with pineapple pieces and some crystallised violets.

To make filling: Beat butter or margarine until soft, add icing sugar and milk. Beat to a smooth cream, and finally add the drained and finely chopped pineapple to the mixture.

To make icing: Put icing sugar in saucepan, add lemon juice and pineapple juice and sufficient water to make a thick coating. Beat thoroughly to make the icing smooth, and stir over a gentle heat for one minute.

13. Abolo

6 cups corn	2 large sweet potatoes
Salt	Abrube leaves

Pound the corn, remove the husks and wash the corn. Boil $3/4$ of the corn, and the raw corn and grind the two together. Peel and boil the sweet potatoes. Mash them and add to the dough. Add salt and a little water, mix well. Take about two tablespoonful and fold into the Abrube leaves. Bake for about one hour.

***Note:** The dough should not be too wet.*

14. Rich Aboodoo

6 cups of corn	2 large sweet potatoes
Groundnuts	Salt $1/2$ lb. beef

Pound the corn, remove the husks and wash. Boil $3/4$ of the corn, add the raw corn and grind the two together. Peel and boil the little water and mix well. Take about two tablespoonful of the dough and fold into the centre some groundnuts and a piece of beef. Wrap in Abrube leaves and bake for about one hour.

15. Cornmeal Muffins

$3/4$ cup cornmeal	2 tablesp. shortening
$1 1/4$ cups flour	A pinch of salt
1 teasp. baking powder	1 egg
1 tablesp. sugar	Milk or water to mix

Sift cornmeal with flour and make as for standard (recipe).

16. Garri Biscuits

1 cig. tin garri	4 ozs. flour
$1 1/2$ ozs. margarine 1 egg	2 ozs. sugar
$1/4$ teasp. salt	1 teasp. baking powder
A little grated nutmeg	
A little milk to mix (if necessary)	

1. Prepare as for Garri Buns (Recipe).
2. Roll out on a floured board to $1/4$ in. thick.
3. Cut into rounds and pinch or mark the edges with a fork.

4. Brush over with beaten white of egg and sugar or with milk.
5. Bake in a moderate oven for about 15 minutes till golden brown.

17. Roasted Cornmeal Biscuits

4 ozs. ground roasted corn or roasted cornmeal	2 eggs
	A pinch of salt
6 ozs. flour	4 ozs. sugar
4 ozs. margarine	Milk to mix of 2 limes
A little grated nutmeg or rinds	

Make as for Garri Biscuits (Recipe 16). Dredge top with fine sugar when cooked.

18. Garri And Groundnut Buns

Prepare as for Garri and Coconut Buns (Recipe 19) using roasted and lightly crushed groundnuts instead of grated coconut.

19. Garri And Coconut Buns

$1/2$ cig. tin garri	2 ozs. sugar

3 ozs. flour	¼ teasp. salt
2 ozs. or 4 tablesp.	1 egg
1 oz. grated butter or margarine	
1 teasp. baking powder	
Milk to mix if necessary	
A little grated nutmeg or coconut cinnamon	

Prepare as for Garri Buns (Recipe 20).

20. Garri Buns

(To make 20 buns)

5 ozs. flour	1 egg
2 ozs. sugar	A pinch of salt
1 cig. tin garri (about 5 ozs.)	
1 teasp. baking powder	
2 ozs. butter or margarine	A little milk

1. Damp garri with a little water.
2. Rub fat into flour, add baking powder, sugar, salt and garri.
2. Beat egg lightly. Add egg and enough milk to make a stiff dough.

4. Pile into heaps on a greased baking tin, use about 1 tablesp. for each bun.
5. Bake in hot oven, for 15–20 minutes.

21. *Chocolate Buns*

To the standard recipe add:

> 1 tablesp. cocoa powder
> 2 ozs. (2 tablesp.) extra sugar
> $1/2$ teasp. vanilla essence

Sift cocoa powder with flour, add essence to egg, and bake in the usual way.

22. *General Rules For Cake-Making*

1. Before starting work, collect all the bowls, spoons and other apparatus needed. It is inconvenient to go back to a drawer or cupboard with floury hands, and a cake mixture should not stand about after beating. Grease cake pans with a saltless fat, e.g., fresh butter, sweet oil, lard or margarine

which has been melted and skimmed. Cake pans may be floured, or if to be used for very rich cakes line them with greased paper.

2. Use good quality ingredients — one bad egg or a little musty flour will ruin a cake.

3. Prepare all ingredients carefully before mixing them together. Wash salt butter. Margarine, which is cheaper, can be used for small buns and economical cakes. Sift flour several times — this not only removes impurities, but mixes air with the flour. Air will help to make the cake light.

Pick and clean currants, sultanas, etc. they may be cleaned by washing and then drying in a clean towel or in the sun, or by rubbing in a little flour which must afterwards be sifted from the currants and thrown away. If wet fruit is used it may make a cake heavy, and the cake will not keep well.

4. Measure ingredients carefully. Do not use too much baking powder (or soda) — this spoils the flavour of a cake.

5. Try to work plenty of air into a cake. Do this by thorough sifting and beating. Air expands when the mixture is baked and this makes the cake rise well.

6. Bake the cake immediately the mixing is finished. If allowed to stand, the air bubbles gradually fall and the baking powder may lose some of its strength.

7. See that the oven is properly heated before putting the cake. (See General Rules for Baking, No. 5, P.). Small buns need a hot oven to brown them quickly. Large cakes need a moderate oven, otherwise the outside is overcooked before the centre is done.

8. Open the oven door as little as possible, and never bang it. Constant opening cools the oven and makes the cake fall.

9. When cooked the cake should be well risen, golden brown (dark brown for a rich fruit cake), firm on top and slightly shrunken away from the side of the tin. When it looks like this and not before, test the centre with a clean warm skewer or knife. If no soft uncooked mixture sticks to the skewer, the cake is done.

10. Do not leave the cake in a draught when it is first taken from the oven. Leave it in the tin for about five minutes, then turn it upside down. Loosen with a knife if necessary. Remove any paper and place right side up on a wire tray. Protect from flies.

23. Cakes, Biscuits And Icing

Ways of making cakes

1. **The Rubbing-in Method**
Flour and shortening (butter, etc.) are mixed together till crumby. This method is good for

rather simple buns and cakes, and is also used for short-crust pastry. (See picture 2).

2. **The Melting or Gingerbread Method**
Shortening is melted and cooked before being mixed with flour. This method is used for fairly plain cakes and hot-water crust pastry, etc.

3. **The Creaming Method**
Shortening and sugar are beaten together till creamy. This is a favourite way of mixing cakes — it is excellent for rich Christmas and wedding cakes, and just as good when used for plain butter-sponge or Madeira cake. See picture 3.

4. **Whisking or Sponging Method**
Eggs and sugar are beaten until stiff and frothy. This method is used for plain sponges which are very light and digestible, but because they contain little or no shortening they get stale very quickly.

24. Ashanti Fowl

1 fowl	2 slices of yam
Salt to taste	8 onions
4 medium-sized pepper	paste tomatoes
Flour	3 ozs. fat
1 cig. tin groundnut	
$1/2$ teasp. ground	

Stuffing

1. Prepare yam, grind pepper, onions and tomatoes.
2. Fry pepper, onions, tomatoes, groundnuts paste and yam.

Fowl

1. Kill chicken and pluck dry.
2. Wash with warm water.
3. Cut off lower half of wings and the feet.
4. Remove the oil bag.
5. Slit down the back and remove back bone;

cut the top part of the neck.

6. Remove the internal organs, being careful not to break the gall-bladder.
7. Loosen flesh and remove leg bones, being careful not to break the skin. Remove the breast bone.
8. Quickly wash all over, lay fat on board and sprinkle with salt.
9. Stuff with prepared stuffing, tie up into shape and dot breast with lard.
10. Grease a deep baking tin or pot, flour chicken lightly and bake or pot roast for $1\frac{1}{4}$–$1\frac{1}{2}$ hours.

25. Baked Ripe Plantain *(Kokototoe)*

| 4 ripe plantains | 1 cig. tin roasted groundnuts |

1. Heat swish oven thoroughly.
2. Peel fully ripe plantains, and tear the skin into strips lengthways.
3. Remove ends of firewood when the oven is hot. Break up glowing embers in the oven into small pieces about the lumps of sugar.

4. Nearly cover embers with plantain skins, and quickly arrange plantain in oven.
5. Rake until golden brown.
6. Serve with roasted groundnuts.

26. Baked Rice Dough (Abolo)

2 cig. tin rice	Water
1 teasp. salt	

1. Steep rice for 10 hours or overnight, drain off water, pound until very fine, and sieve.
2. Divide rice flour into three parts and cook one part.
3. Mix with raw portion, and add water to soften dough; leave overnight to rise.
4. Warm fresh plantain leaves and cut into suitable pieces for wrapping.
5. Divide into three or four portions and wrap each in plantain leaves.
6. Tie with string made from mid-rib or leaves, and bake in a hot oven for 45 minutes.
7. Cool and serve.

27. Baked Corn Dough

> 3 cig. tins corn dough
> 1 tablesp. flour or sweet potatoes
> 1 teasp. salt
> $1/2 - 3/4$ pint water

1. Partly cook half the dough to make ohu or aflata, add salt.
2. Peel, wash and grate potatoes.
3. Mix cooked and uncooked dough together, add flour or grated potatoes and a little water.
4. Leave to rise for 6–8 hours.
5. Wrap in clean plantain or "abolo baa" leaves.
6. Bake in hot oven for half an hour.
7. Serve with stew, fried fish or roasted meat.

Note: *Sweet potato flour may be added instead of wheat flour.*

28. Rich Baked Plantain Dough *(Rich Ofam)*

> 1 cig. tin rice or fresh corn
> $3/4$–1 pint palm oil and 1 gill dough or fresh corn meal

water or 2 pints palm-nut	
1½ cig. tins roasted groundnuts	liquid
	8 onions
8 ripe plantains	2 teasp. ground pepper
2 tablesp. flour	1 teasp. salt
1 piece root ginger	8 eggs (soft boiled)

Method I

1. Wash and soak rice overnight. Grind and sieve finely.
2. Pound the ripe plantains well, mix with rice flour or corn dough.
3. Grind and add ginger and onions, add pepper, palm oil and salt.
4. Skin and crush roasted groundnuts roughly, add to the mixture.
5. Shell eggs carefully.
6. Grease tins well with palm oil and put in half the mixture. Gently drop an egg in each and fill tin two-thirds way up.
7. Bake in a moderately hot oven for $1-1\frac{1}{2}$ hours.

Method II

Prepare as above, using beans instead of groundnuts.

To prepare beans:
1. Pick, wash and soak beans overnight.
2. Boil till soft. Mash and add to the mixture

OR

1. Pick, wash and dry beans.
2. Pound and sieve into a meal.
3. Add this to the mixture.

Note: *Where bean meal is used, add $1/_2$ pint more water or palm-nut liquid, to make a softer mixture.*

29. Baked Plantain Dough

> 2 cig. tins rice or fresh corn
> 1 gill water and $1/_4$ – 1 pint
> dough or fresh cornmeal
> palm oil or 2 pints palm nut

10 ripe plantains	liquid
1 piece root ginger	6 onions
2 teasp. ground pepper	1 teasp. salt
2 tablesp. flour (optional)	

1. Soak rice overnight, grind and sieve it.
2. Pound the ripe plantains smoothly, mix with ground rice or corn dough.
3. Add ground pepper, ground ginger, salt, ground onions and palm oil.
4. Allow to stand for 2–3 hours.
5. Grease tins well with palm oil, fill two-thirds full with mixture.
6. Bake in a hot oven for 30–45 minutes.

30. Baked Cornmeal And Plantain *(Apiti)*

4 cig. tins cornmeal	2 teasp. salt
6 ripe plantains	2 teasp. pepper

Method I

1. Pound ripe plantains till smooth, add to cornmeal and mix in salt and pepper.

2. Put about 4 tablesp. mixture on to dry plantain leaves.
3. Bake in a hot oven for about 30 minutes till golden brown.
4. Serve hot or cold as a sweet.

Method II

Use corn dough instead of cornmeal, and add about $1/2$ pint water. Make as for Method I, and serve cold with roasted groundnuts.

Method III

1. Prepare as for Baked Cornmeal and Plantain, Method II.
2. Add palm oil.
3. Bake in a hot oven for 20 minutes.

Fried Foods

Do not eat too much fried foods.

Fry foods with a little amount of oil.

Note the following frying methods used in this Section.

1. *Dry Frying:*

No fat is placed in the pan, as the food contains sufficient oil for frying, e.g. bacon, *eburow na nkatse* (groundnuts and corn.)

2. Shallow Frying:

Sufficient fat is used to prevent the food from sticking to the bottom and burning. When the food is brown on one side it is turned over and browned on the other, e.g., fried plantain.

3. Deep Frying:

Sufficient fat is used to entirely cover the food, e.g., kakro, skull.

31. Eburow Ne Nkatse *(Nkyewe)*

1 cupful corn	Salt
½ cupful groundnuts	

Fry corn in dry pot. When slightly brown, add groundnuts and wet salt. Fry for about 15 minutes. — Serve cold.

32. Akrakro

2½ lbs. ripe plantain	1 lb. dough
Palm oil, onions	Pepper, salt

Peel the plantain. Beat well in a mortar to free it from lumps. Mix well with the dough until it becomes thick. Add the prepared pepper, salt and onion. Mix well. Heat the palm oil in a pan. When hot, roll a piece of dough into a ball and fry until quite brown. Continue to fry in the same way till the dough is used up. Serve hot with pepper paste.

33. Tetare

1 lb. ripe plantain	$1/2$ lb. dough,
flour or ground rice	Onions
Salt	1 pt. water
Pepper	1 bottle palm oil

Clean and pound the plantain until quite soft. Mix in dough, ground pepper and onions. Add salt. Take two or three tablespoonful of the mixture and fry in hot oil.

Note: *Do not have the mixture too wet or it will stick to the pan. Serve with beans.*

34. Kenan with Gravy

6 herrings or pieces of fresh fish
3 tablesp. flour $1/2$ teasp. salt
(Twi & Fante method Oil or lard for frying only)

For Gravy

$1/2$ teasp. pepper   8 onions
$1/2$ teasp. salt $1/2$ gill vegetable oil
6 tomatoes

1. Scale, clean and wash fish, cut into suitable pieces, or leave herrings whole.
2. Rub salt into fish or dip in salt water.
3. Dry slightly and dip in flour (optional).
4. Fry in smoking hot fat until brown on both sides.
5. Strain and keep oil for future use.
6. Make gravy and serve with kenkey or abolo.

Note: *Herrings are sometimes cut along the sides and stuffed with ground pepper, onions and salt.*

35. Meensa or Millet Cake

> 3 cig. tins millet

1. Wet the millet and pound it lightly to lossen husks.
2. Add water to remove husks.
3. Strain and keep the water.
4. Pound and sieve one half.
6. Add enough of the strained water to the other half to mix to the consistency of porridge and boil until thick.
6. Add the sieved millet and enough strained water to mix to a pouring consistency.
7. Leave overnight to ferment.
8. Shallow fry and serve warm.

36. Quick Chicken and Mushroom

> 3 tablespoons vegetable oil
>
> 4 uncooked joints of chicken
>
> ground mushroom, garden eggs, salt and some pepper.

Heat oil in frying pan, put in chicken joints, turn them now and then while cooking slowly (about

15 minutes) over gentle heat until golden. Transfer joints to casserole. Drain surplus fat from frying pan, then pour in soup, and heat, stirring until boiling. Pour over chicken, cover casserole and cook over fire for 30–40 minutes. Season with pepper.

37. Saasee Special

Fry button mushrooms (saasee) gently in lard until just tender. Dip in salted water. Serve sprinkled with raw chopped onion and pepper with cooked yam. Eat on cocktail sticks.

38. Chicken Pancake

> 1 oz. plain flour, good pinch salt, 1 egg, 1 pint milk, 1 teaspoon corn oil for frying, 1 teacup diced cooked chicken, 2 oz. chopped fried mushrooms (domo or nkyemire) salt and pepper.

Sift flour and salt into basin. Separate egg yolk from white, then beat egg yolk, milk and 1 teaspoon corn oil into flour to make smooth batter, keep egg white. Add diced chicken and chopped mushrooms to batter. Season. Then whisk egg white stiffly and fold into mixture. Heat about 1 dessertspoon corn oil in strong frying pan. Place spoonful of pancake mixture well in pan, cook over moderate heat 2–3 minutes, then turn and cook the other side. Drain on crumpled kitchen paper and keep hot.

39. Baby Rissoles

Mix $1/2$ lb. minced veal and $1/2$ minced pork together with 1 small chopped onion, 1 dessertspoon of flour and seasoning. Bind mixture with 1 small beaten egg. Use a teaspoon dipped in hot butter to form into small balls. Fry gently in hot fat, turning until brown and cooked through. Drain, top each rissole with a small piece of beet-root secured with cocktail stick. Makes: about 36.

40. Fried Vegetables
(General rules)

1. Peel, wash and cut up as follows:
   Sweet potato and cocoyam — cut into thin slices.
   Yam — cut into $1/4$–$1/2$ in. slices and then into 4–6 strips.
   Plantain (ripe or partly ripe) — cut lengthwise into 2–3 pieces.
2. If preferred, soak sweet potatoes, cocoyams and yams in salted water for half an hour, then drain and dry well. Soak plantain only for 2–3 minutes.
3. Heat oil until smoking hot, then fry a few slices at a time to avoid lowering temperature of the oil.
4. When golden brown outside and soft inside, drain well and serve hot.
5. If not previously soaked in salted water, sprinkle with salt.

41. Akpete

6 cig. tins corn	Kernel oil for frying
1/2 lb. sugar	2 teasp. salt
4 tablesp. flour	

1. Soak corn overnight, and grind the following day.
2. Mix with a little water, add salt, sugar and flour.
   Stand aside for half an hour.
3. Make into small balls, and fry in deep fat until golden brown.
4. Serve hot or cold.

42. Garri Kaklo

1 cig. tin garri	1/2 teasp. salt
4 tablesp. flour	1/4 teasp. pepper
1 coconut or 1 cig. tin	1 gill water
Vegetable oil 1/4 (except palm oil) for frying groundnuts	

1. Mix garri and water. Stand for 15 minutes.
2. Add sieved flour and seasoning and mix well.

3. Add more water if necessary to form a fairly soft dough.
4. Make into balls and fry till golden brown.
5. Serve with coconut or roasted groundnuts.

43. Nkye Mmire Or Domo (Special)

> 1 large slice of cooked yam, 1 egg,
> salt and pepper, fat for frying
> $1/_4$ lb. small mushrooms, 1oz. butter
> 3–4 tablespoons hot water

Dip cooked yam in egg whisked together with salt and pepper. Fry in hot fat until golden both sides. Wash, dry and lightly fry mushrooms in palm oil or lard, add 3–4 tablespoons hot water, cover with lid and continue cooking until tender. Serve on top of prepared fried yam.

44. Shrimp Special

> Lard, 3 level tablespoons plain flour,
> 1 can (3$^3/_4$oz.) shrimps or prawns,
> 1 small can (5oz.) garden eggs or 1 cup cooked peas,
> pepper, salt, 1 egg yolk, 2 pieces tomatoes (optional).

Put lard in a small saucepan, then stir in flour and blend well. Gradually add tomatoes, pepper and salt, bring to the boil and stir mixture for three minutes. Add shrimps or prawns (reserving a few for decoration) and drained peas. Lower heat and carefully stir in egg yolk until slightly thickened. Serve with freshly made hot buttered roasted yam, plantain or cassava chips.

45. Bankye Krakro

Cassava	Vegetable oil for frying
Salt	

1. Scrub, peel and wash cassava.
2. Grate and squeeze out the juice.
3. Add salt and shape into balls (2 tablesp. each).
4. Fry in hot oil.
5. Serve with coconut.

46. Ntomo Krakro

4 sweet potatoes	$1/4$ teasp. salt

1 tablesp. flour	Water (or milk if preferred)
2 large eggs	Bread crumbs for coating
2 tablesp. butter or fat	
Oil for frying	

1. Peel, boil and mash sweet potatoes.
2. Beat eggs and add rest of the ingredients.
3. Add enough liquid to mix into a fairly soft dough.
4. Make into flat cakes. Coat with beaten eggs and breadcrumbs.
5. Fry in hot fat until golden brown.
6. Drain well and serve hot with meat or fish stew.

47. Akla

Method I

2 cig. tins dried beans	1 beer bottle
1 teasp. salt	About ½ pint water
vegetable oil or lard for frying	

1. Pick, wash and soak beans overnight.
2. Pound and grind until smooth, and mix with water to thick batter consistently.
3. Add salt and beat well, allow to stand for 30 minutes.
4. Fry in spoonfuls in hot oil until golden brown.
5. Serve hot or cold with akasa or abolo.

Method II

To the above add:

$1/_2$ teasp. ground pepper	4 onions
$1/_2$ teasp. ground ginger	2 tablesp. flour

1. Prepare as for Method I.
2. Fry and serve hot or cold with garri, or abolo, or yakayake.

48. Kyekyire Krako

$1^1/_2$ cig. tins ablemamu	2 teasp. ground pepper or
6 ripe plantains	1 teasp. ground pepper
6 onions	1 teasp. ground ginger

2 teasp. salt	Palm oil or kernel oil for frying

1. Pound plantains and mix with ablemamu.
2. Grind onion and salt together, add pepper and mix with other ingredients.
3. Form into balls and fry in hot oil till brown.
4. Drain well and serve hot.

49. Sweet Corn Dough Cakes

1 lb. fresh corn dough	4 tablesp. water
2 tablesp. flour	1 teasp. salt
Kernel oil or lard for frying	2 tablesp. sugar

Method I

1. Mix corn dough, salt, sugar, flour and water to make a stiff dough.
2. Form into oval shapes with hand (about size of a big egg).
3. Fry in smoking hot oil until brown and cooked.
4. Serve hot or cold as sweet.

Method II

1. Partly cook half the dough to make ohu.
2. Mix cooked and uncooked dough together with flour, salt and water, cover and leave overnight.
3. Next morning, add sugar, form into oval shapes (about size of a big egg).
4. Fry in smoking hot oil until brown and cooked.
5. Serve hot or cold as sweet —
    (a) by itself or
    (b) with roasted groundnuts or
    (c) with coconut.

50. More Krakro

4 ripe plantains	10 peppers or 1 teasp.
2 cig. tins corn dough	4 onions
ground pepper and	1 teasp. salt
$1/2$ teasp ground ginger.	
Kernel oil or palm oil for frying	
ground pepper, or $1/2$ teasp ...	

1. Pound plantain until free from lumps.
2. Mix plantains and corn dough, add pepper, onions and salt, and allow to rise for half an hour.
3. Form into balls and fry a few at a time in smoking hot oil till brown.
4. Drain well and serve hot.

51. Pancakes with Ground Rice and Flour

2 rip plantains	$1/_4$ pint water
$1/_2$ tablesp. flour	1 teasp. salt
3 tablesp. ground rice	1 teasp. ground pepper
3 onions	Palm oil for frying

(b) Corn Dough Pancakes

As for Ground Rice Pancakes using 1 cig. tin corn dough.

Note: *If plantain are not fully ripe, add 1–2 tablesp. sugar or mixture.*

Method II

1. Wash and steep rice overnight, grind finely and mix with water.
2. Beat plantains till free from lumps, and mix with ground rice and flour or corn dough.
3. Grind onions, pepper and salt together, add to plantain mixture, and stand aside to ferment for two hours or longer.
4. Fry by spoonfuls in smoking hot oil until both sides are brown and the inside is cooked.
5. Serve hot with pea or bean stew or stewed beans.

Method III

1. Grind pepper, onions and salt together.
2. Pound half the plantain and mix well in bowl with the water.
3. Add flour, ground rice or corn dough, pepper, onions and salt, mix well.
4. Set aside for six hours or overnight.
5. Pound remainder of plantain and add to fermented mixture.

6. Fry in very hot oil, measuring 1¹/₂ serving spoonfuls into the oil at a time.
7. Fry until brown on both sides.
8. Serve hot.

Roasted Foods

Note the Rules for Roasting used in this Section:

1. Have a good bright fire, or a hot oven at first.
2. Weigh meat before roasting.
3. Allow 15 minutes to the 1 lb. and 15 minutes over for beef. Allow 20 minutes to the lb. and 20 minutes over for mutton. Allow 25 minutes to the lb. and 25 minutes over for stuffed meats.
4. Use only the best joints for roasting.
5. Have a hot oven for first 10 minutes, to form a coating on the meat, then cook gently.

6. Baste frequently.
7. Serve with gravy.

52. To Make Gravy

Pour the fat from the pan, leaving about one tablespoonful. Add boiling water, salt and pepper and boil well stirring all the time. Serve in a hot gravy boat or serve round meat.

53. Brown Gravy

Remove the roast from the pan and pour off most of the fat. Put over the fire and add $1/2$ ozs. flour and stir until it browns. Add water and stir until it boils. Season well and boil for five minutes. Strain and serve.

54. Roast Duck

1 fowl, duck	1 oz. butter	Pepper
Salt	2 thick slices of yam	
Lard or fat for basting		

Pluck, singe and trust the bird for roasting. Boil the yam and mash while still hot. Parboil and chop the onions, add to the mashed yam. Add the butter, pepper and salt. Mix well, stuff the fowl, roasting tin with lard or dripping on top. Cover with a greased paper. Place in a hot oven for first 10 minutes. Lower the heat and cook slowly. Baste frequently. Cook for $1^1/_2$ to $2^1/_2$ hours according to the size. Serve with brown gravy.

55. Pineapple Meringue

> 3 egg whites, pinch salt, 6 ozs. caster sugar,
> 3 level teaspoons cornflour. Filling and decoration:
> 1 large can pineapple, $^1/_2$ pint of whipped double cream,
> glace cherries.

Whisk egg whites with salt until stiff, then whisk in 3 teaspoons of sugar and beat until satiny and stiff enough to stand in peaks. Fold in rest of sugar and cornflour. Line 2 baking sheets with oiled grease-proof paper. Then spread equal-size thick rounds of meringue mixture on each tin. Sprinkle tops with a little extra caster sugar. Bake in a very slow oven (200 deg. F. — Mark $1/2$) for 3–4 hours or until dry and set. Remove the paper from base of meringue rounds one hour before end of cooking time and turn rounds upside down. Cool on wire rack, then add filling and decoration. Serve 4–6.

To fill and decorate: Drain and chop pineapple, keeping a few pieces for decoration, and place on one meringue half; spread with whipped cream and top with other meringue half. Decorate top of the meringue with pineapple pieces.

56. Chicken With Pineapple

A 3–4 lb. roasting chicken, salt, 4–5 tablespoons cooking oil, 1 tablespoonful of pepper.

Stuffing: $1\frac{1}{2}$ ozs. butter, 2 ozs. green sweet pepper, salt, grated rind, $1/2$ lemon, 1 large fresh pineapple — cut into rings.

Remove giblets from chicken. Sprinkle inside of chicken lightly with salt. Pack prepared stuffing loosely into neck cavity, secure neck cavity with skewer. Place in roasting tin, brush chicken with a little of the oil. Sprinkle on pepper. Pour remaining oil into bottom of tin. Cook in pre-heated moderately hot oven allowing 20 minutes to the pound and 20 minutes over. Baste chicken from time to time during cooking. Heat pineapple rings left over from stuffing in oven 10 minutes before serving. Arrange the chicken on serving dish with pineapple rings.

To make stuffing: Melt butter in pan, add bread crumbs, cook 1–2 minutes. Add walnuts, seasoning, lemon rind and 2 rings drained and chopped pineapple.

57. Roast Meat or Fowl

Meat	Salt
Onions	Vegetable oil or lard
Pepper	Tomatoes

1. Wash and trim meat. Grind pepper, onion and salt together and rub all over meat. In the case of a fowl, stuff with ground pepper, onions, salt and tomatoes.

2. Put into tin or clay pot, put oil at bottom of pot.
3. Bake in a hot swish oven, according to size of meat, allowing 20 minutes for every lb. of meat and 20 minutes over for the piece.
4. During baking, open oven once and turn meat.
5. Make gravy, serve meat with kenkey, abolo or banku.

58. Roasted Corn And Groundnut Meal (Sale)

1 cig. tin corn	4 ozs. sugar
1/2 cig. tin groundnuts	1/2 teasp. salt

1. Roast corn and groundnuts alternatively until brown.
2. Spread groundnuts and corn to cool.
3. Pound the corn in a mortar, add groundnuts, salt and sugar, pound and sieve.
4. Serve in a plate.

59. Roasted Corn And Groundnuts (Nkyewe)

1 cig. tin corn	Salt
Water	1 cig. tin roasted groundnuts

Method I

1. Heat pot and roast corn over slow fire till golden brown.
2. Pour into salted water and allow to soak for 20 minutes or longer.
3. Drain off water and heat corn until dry.
4. Serve with roasted groundnuts.

Method II (For crisper result)

1. Roast corn.
2. Reduce heat and sprinkle salted water on corn gradually while still hot. Continue cooking until quite dry.

Note: Roast groundnuts and corn alternately in clean hot sand to give even result.

60. Mashed Roasted Cocoyam (Sasa)

Method I

2 big cocoyams	About ½ pint palm oil
½ teasp. salt	

1. Roast cocoyam on smokeless embers till done.
2. Scrape off burnt skin.
3. Cut into pieces. Mash well and add salt.
4. Mix with palm oil.
5. Heat and serve.

Method II

2 big cocoyams	2 tomatoes
½ teasp. salt	4 onions
½ teasp. ground pepper	½ pint palm oil

1. Roast cocoyams and scrape off burnt skin.
2. Cut into pieces.
3. Prepare and slice onions and tomatoes.
4. Fry in palm oil, adding pepper.
5. Mash cocoyams well and add salt.

6. Mix all ingredients.
7. Re-heat if necessary and serve hot.

61. Roasted Cassava Meal

| 2 sticks cassava | Salt to taste |

1. Peel and wash cassava well. Grate finely.
2. Put in a clean white cloth and squeeze out all juice.
3. Crumble, sieve and mix with crushed salt.
4. Heat a tatale frying dish or a thick frying pan slowly and sprinkle on some mixture.
5. Cook until golden brown on one side. Turn and cook the other side till dry and brown.
6. Serve hot or cold either alone or with roasted groundnuts, coconut or corn-dough.

62. Roasted Stuffed Cocoyam (Amankani Asombrofi)

1 big cocoyam	2 onions
$1/2$ teasp. salt	About 1 gill palm oil
1 teasp. ground pepper	1 smoked fish (optional)

1. Roast cocoyam on smokeless embers till done.
2. Scrape off burnt skin.
3. Cut off a lid and keep.
4. Scrape out some of the inner flesh to form a big hole.
5. Prepare and cut onions, grind, adding salt and pepper. Fry in hot palm oil.
6. Pour mixture in hole and fill with scraped out cocoyam. Put on lid.
7. Remove hot embers from stove and stand cocoyam upright in warm stove and allow oil to soak slowly and thoroughly into cocoyam.
8. Serve hot.

Note: *This is especially suitable for use on journeys; it is prepared the night before.*

63. Roasted Plantain (Ripe Or Unripe)

1. Peel and wash plantains, cut in halves and slice lengthwise.
2. Roast on slow open embers or on top of roasting wire.

3. Serve hot with roasted groundnuts. If plantains are unripe, serve with groundnuts or palm-oil stew.

Steamed Foods

Steaming

Note different methods of Steaming in this Section:

Food may be steamed:

1. In a saucepan with boiling water to come half up the basin.
2. In a steamer on the top of a saucepan of boiling water.
3. On a covered plate over a saucepan of boiling water.

4. In a double saucepan.

Rules for Steaming:

1. The water must be boiling before use, and kept boiling all the time.
2. The water must not touch the food.
3. As the water boils away more boiling water must be added.
4. Steamer should be provided with a tight fitting lid, to retain the heat and steam.
5. If a basin is to be used it should be greased, and also the paper cover to keep out the steam.

64. Steamed Fish

| Fish | $1/_2$ oz. butter |
| Pepper | Salt |

Remove the skin and bone from the fish. Wash and dry, sprinkle with pepper and salt. Grease a plate and put it over a saucepan of boiling water. Put the seasoned fish on the plate and cover with another plate. Allow to steam for about 25 minutes. Serve with white sauce.

65. Etsew

| 1 lb. dough | Water | Salt |

Boil the water and the salt. When the water is boiled, add the dough in small pieces. Mix well with a wooden spoon. Add more water as required. Mix again until quite smooth. When well cooked, take pot from the fire and have a basin of cold water ready. Put dough on a flat plate. Dip the hands in water and take about 3 oz. of the dough and shape. Put on a dish and cover to keep warm. Continue until all the dough is used up. Serve with Forowe or Akatsewa Stew. *See* page ..

Note: *White Etsew is made in the same way except the dough is first mixed with cold water and then cooked, the salt being added to the cold water.*

66. Corn and Sugar (Kyekyerewa)

2 cig. tins corn
1 teasp. crushed salt
$1/2$ lb. granulated or crushed lump sugar
Corn shooks or plantain leaves

Method I

1. Pound and husk corn. Wash and soak overnight or for eight hours.
2. Prepare a platform of sticks and shooks in pot, add and boil water.
3. Mix sugar and salt with corn.
4. Wrap ladlefuls of prepared corn in corn shooks or dry plantain leaves and tie securely.
5. Place parcels over the prepared platform of sticks and leaves.
6. Steam for 3–4 hours.
7. Serve hot or cold.

Method II

1. Prepare as for Method I leaving out sugar.
2. Serve with coconut or roasted groundnut.

67. Komi

> 2 cig. tins soured corn dough
> ½ pint boiling water   ½ teasp. salt
> Corn shooks and stalks

1. Divide corn dough into two portions.
2. Put water on to boil and add salt.
3. Put one ball into boiling water for a few seconds.
4. Mix well with a wooden stirrer to make into aflatta, ohu or half-cooked banku.
5. Add aflatta to uncooked dough, mix well into smooth paste.
6. Divide into portions, wrap each in clean, wet corn shooks.
7. Cover bottom of iron pot with strips of corn shooks and stalks; add boiling water.
8. Arrange balls of kenkey on the corn stalks.
9. Cover with heavy cloth or corn leaves and a basin.
10. Steam for two hours, until soft and light.
11. Serve hot or cold with stew, soup or fried fish.

Note: *Sometimes the husks (skins) of the corn are removed before it is ground; this makes smoother, finer kenkey.*

68. Dokon Or Fante Kenkey

1. Ferment corn dough for two days only.
2. Steam in plantain leaves.
3. Do not use salt, otherwise make as Twi Kenkey.

69. Steamed Cassava Dough

4 cig. tins cassava dough	1 teasp. salt

Method I

1. Boil some water and fit top of pot with a steamer.
2. Seal edges with a paste of cassava dough.
3. Line steamer with corn shooks or clean white cloth.
4. Sieve cassava dough and mix with salt, fill steamer with dough, cover and steam for $1/2$–1 hour.

5. Remove and serve with palm-nut soup, fried fish or stew.

Method II

After cooking, crumble steamed cassava dough and mix with about $1/_2$ pint palm oil.

70. Steamed Cornmeal *(Kpokpoi)*

> 5 cig. tins cornmeal or dry corn
> 6 onions   4 okros
> 1 teasp. salt   About 1 pint palm oil
> Corn leaves (shooks)

1. Dry soured corn dough, or prepare dry corn by soaking for three days in a little water and then grind it.
2. Rub the dough lightly with finger tips to make into fine powder.
3. Place clay steamer (Ntaso) over pot of boiling water, and seal edges with paste of dough.
4. Line steamer with strips of corn leaves or clean white cloth.
5. Sprinkle dough on to the leaves, and allow to

cook over steam until the colour changes to light yellow – about three-quarters of an hour.
6. Boil okros and mash with salt.
7. Fry chopped onions in a little palm oil.
8. Lightly mix cooked cornmeal with onions, salt and half the okros and palm oil.
9. Put neatly in a dish and dress with palm oil and remaining okros.
10. Serve with palm-nut soup.

71. Steamed Sweet Kenkey (Dokompa)

8 cig. tins corn	3 teasp. salt
$1/2$ lb. sugar	About 2 pints water
2 thin slices of yam	plantain leaves
$1/2$ cig. tin flour	
4 sweet potatoes or Dry corn shooks or fresh	

1. Pick, wash and soak corn for three days.
2. Make into corn dough.
3. Partly cook half the dough into ohu, and mix with uncooked dough.
4. Boil and mash yam or sweet potatoes, add

rest of ingredients and mix well.
5. Soften with water to a soft consistency, and allow to stand for eight hours.
6. Heat water and prepare pot for steaming.
7. Wrap mixture in leaves, and steam for four hours.
8. Serve hot or cold.

72. Plantain Kenkey (Akankye)

8 very ripe plantains	8 tablesp. unripe plantain
2 teasp. ground pepper	meal (amada)
1 teasp. salt	

1. Beat the ripe plantains till free from lumps.
2. Mix the beaten plantain with plantain meal. Add ground pepper and salt, and mix well.
3. Allow to rise in a warm place for six hours.
4. Roll in plantain leaves, and arrange in a pot on a platform of sticks and leaves, and steam for 4–5 hours.

73. Tuubaani *(Steamed Cow-Peas)*

2 cig. tins bean	Large leaves to wrap
A pinch of kawa (salt petre)	

1. Grind beans into flour.
2. Put water on fire to boil.
3. Mix the powdered beans into a paste and add kawa.
4. Wrap small servings of paste in leaves.
5. Arrange pieces of stick in the boiler and cover with a sponge or leaves; then arrange leaves containing bean paste on top.
6. Steam for one hour.
7. Serve hot with gravy.

74. Wasawasa *(Steamed Yam Flour)*

2 cig. tins yam flour (yam heads are used)

1. Place a perforated pot over a pot containing boiling water. Arrange sticks and sponge in the upper pot.
2. Wet the yam flour. Put a little at a time in a calabash and shake the calabash from side to

side until the flour forms small beads.
3. Sprinkle the mixture on the sponge and steam for one hour.
4. Serve with gravy.

75. Cassava Yakayeke

Cassava	Salt
Ground corn	Sugar (if liked)

Peal and grate the cassava. Put into a sack and squeeze out the water. Dry the cassava. Sieve it and add salt and the ground corn. Mix well. Take about three tablespoonfuls at a time and steam. Serve with fried fish or stew.

76. Etew Yakayeke

Dough	Okro
Ground corn	Salt

Dry the dough. Add salt and the ground corn. Mix well and sieve and steam. Cut the Okro into pieces and boil. Add gradually to the steamed yakayeke. Mix well and serve with palm oil soup.

Boiled Foods

Vitamin C is easily destroyed when over boiled so remember not to boil vegetables excessively.

77. Emo Dokon

5 cig. tins rice flour	Water
¼ lb. beef	Seasoning

1. Divide rice flour into three parts and cook one part well.
2. Mix with raw portion, add water and mix to a dropping consistency.
3. Leave overnight to allow dough to rise.

4. Make into balls and enclose a piece of seasoned beef in each.
5. Warm fresh plantain leaves on open fire and arrange ready to hold mixture.
6. Wrap balls in leaves and tie with string made from mid-rib of leaves.
7. Boil in a large quantity of water for 1–2 hours.
8. Drain off water and dry kenkey in a basket.
9. Remove leaves and serve hot.

78. Ntebrefua

Prepare as for mashed yam and eggs I and II using unripe or partly ripe plantains instead of yam.

79. Akapinkyi

4 ripe or unripe plantains or a mixture of both	$1/2$ cig. tin palm oil
	1 teasp. salt
3 smoked fish herring size?	1 teasp. ground pepper

Method I

1. Boil or bake plantains without skins.
2. Pound or mash
3. Grind plantain and add salt and pepper.
4. Wash and break up fish, add oil and mix with plantain.
5. Heat slowly for about 10 minutes; stir well.
6. Serve hot.

Method II

Make as for Method I, but in place of fish, use 1 cig. tin roasted crushed groundnuts, and instead of ground pepper, use $1/2$ teasponful ground ginger.

80. Favourite Curry

> 1 lb. raw beef, mutton or veal
> 2 tablespoons dripping
> 2 small onions
> 2–4 teaspoons curry powder
> 1–2 teaspoons curry paste
> $1/2$ pint stock or water, pepper

1 tablespoon flour

$1/2$ lb. long grain rice, salt

1 tomato

Cut meat into neat pieces then lightly fry in melted fat in saucepan until brown all over. Remove meat, add peeled and chopped onions to fat and cook until golden but not brown. Stir in curry powder and paste; cook, stirring, for 2–3 minutes. Stir in flour and when blended, add stock or water. Bring to boil, stirring, add meat, tomatoes and pepper. Cover and cook gently, stirring now and then, for $1 1/2$ hours or until meat is tender. Add more stock if necessary.

Prepare rice as follows: Rinse first in cold water, cook in large pan of boiling water for about 12 minutes, forking occasionally. Drain in colander, rinse with water. Stand the colander over pan of steaming water, cover with cloth for 2 minutes till rice is dry and fluffy.

Serve curry with freshly boiled rice and side dish and sliced bananas and pine apples.

81. Garri Jollof

2 cig. tins garri	8 onions
4 big tomatoes	1/2 teasp. salt
4 eggs or 1 tin sardines, or	1/4 teasp. pepper
1/4 tin corned beef, or	2 eggs
Vegetable oil for frying	corned beef
and sardines, or 2 eggs and	
About 1 gill water	

1. Mix garri and salted water.
2. Prepare and cut up onions and tomatoes, and fry in hot fat.
3. Add pepper, garri, salt and lightly beaten eggs.
4. Heat and serve hot.

Note: *When using sardines or corned beef, fry with onions and tomatoes before adding garri.*

82. Egg Curry With Rice

6 oz. long grain rice,	salt
1 oz. margarine,	1 onion,
Pepper	1 rounded teaspoon

> 1 level tablespoon plain flour, curry powder,
>
> $1/2$ level teaspoon curry paste
>
> $1/2$ pint hot water, Tomatoes
>
> 1 tablespoon groundnuts,
>
> 3 large freshly cooked hardboiled eggs

Rinse rice in cold water, cook in large pan of boiling salted water for about 12 minutes, forking occasionally, until just tender. Drain and rinse through with hot water. Stand the rice over pan of gently steaming water, cover with cloth and steam 2 minutes till dry and fluffy. Meanwhile melt margarine in small saucepan. Stir in small peeled chopped onion, tomatoes and pepper. Cook for 2 minutes, stirring. Mix in curry powder and flour, cook for further minutes. Remove from heat. Gradually blend in curry, chopped groundnuts. Return pan to heat bring to boil, simmer gently 3 minutes, stirring. Arrange border of cooked rice on serving dish. Place halved hot eggs in centre.

83. Oto

> 5 lb. yam (or 1 yam from 6 in. to 9 in. long)

> 1 cig. tin palm oil,
> 1 teasp. salt, 5 eggs.

Method I

1. Peel, wash and cut yam into small pieces.
2. Boil in salt water until soft.
3. Remove and mash yam, add salt and palm oil.
4. Serve hot with hard-boiled eggs.

Note: *Sometimes yolk of boiled eggs is mashed with the mixture.*

Method II

Ingredients as above plus

> 2 tomatoes, $1/2$ teaspoonful ground pepper.
> 4 onions

1. Finely chop onions and tomatoes
2. Heat palm oil and fry vegetables.
3. Mash yam, add oil, vegetables and salt.
4. Serve hot with hard-boiled eggs.

Note: Both these recipes are used at Twi festivals, especially those connected with twins.

84. Twi Kenkey

Prepare mixture as for Emo Dokon but allow to stand for 6–8 hours before forming into balls.

85. Akoto

4 big river crabs	1 pint water
1 teasp. salt	

Method

1. Kill crabs and wash carefully. Remove eye and under flap.
2. Put in boiling water, and salt and boil for 10 minutes.
3. Reduce heat and simmer for 45 minutes.
4. Drain crabs and serve with kenkey.

Dressing

> 1 teasp. ground pepper
> 2 onions
> 1 tomato
> ³/₄ teasp. salt
> 1 tablesp. water

1. Prepare and grind onions and tomatoes. Add salt, pepper and water.
2. Serve raw or simmer mixture for 10 minutes with crabs and kenkey.

86. Ampesi

> Yam, plantain, cassava, sweet potato, or cocoyam, water, salt.

Method

1. Wash and peel vegetable, cut into pieces.
2. Put to cook in boiling water or in cold for old vegetables.
3. Add salt, boil until soft. Drain off water.
4. Serve with garden egg stew, spinach stew or palm-nut stew.

87. Fufu

Cassava, yam, plantain, or cocoyam may be used. (And except in case of cassava may not be mixed together.)

Water, salt (if the fufu is to be kept for more than one hour).

1. Prepare and wash vegetable.
2. Put into saucepan, cover with water, boil until soft and allow to cool after straining off water.
3. Wash fufu pot and stick.
4. Put the cooked vegetable into a mortar, a little at a time and with the cut side of vegetable uppermost. Beat a little, then remove from the mortar.
5. When all has been beaten a little, return it to the mortar and beat until soft and free from lumps.
6. Turn the fufu over, while beating with clean wet hand.
7. Shape into balls and serve in warm dish.
8. While beating the fufu, keep the food pro-

tected as much as possible from flies and dust.

9. If fufu is to be kept for several hours, add a little salt when beating.

88. Nyoma

> 6 medium-sized yams
> $3/4$ lb. meat or 3 dried
> 1 teasp. ground pepper
> 1 teasp. salt
> 1 cig. tin palm oil or lard
> Small piece salt beef or salt herrings (optional)

1. Peel yams, wash and cut them into $1/2$-inch pieces.
2. Cook slowly in water. Cut the meat or fish (if used) into small pieces, and cook with yam.
3. When yam is soft, add palm oil or lard, salt and pepper.
4. Mix well and serve hot.

Note: *Cocoyam or cassava may be used. Beans may be added if desired.*

89. Kyekyirebetu

2 ripe plantains
$1/2$ teasp. salt
$1/2$ cig. tin roasted corn meal
$1/2$ cig. tin palm oil
$1/2$ teasp. ground pepper

Method I

1. Peel and wash plantains, and boil till soft.
2. Mash, and add salt, pepper and palm oil.
3. Mix well, heat, form into balls and serve.

Method II

Prepare as in Method I, using roasted ripe plantains instead of boiled ones.

90. Kokonte Akankye

1 cig. tin cassava meal
4 ripe plantains
1 cig. tin palm oil
1 teasp. ground pepper
1 teasp. salt

Method I

1. Peel and pound ripe plantains.
2. Add and mix in kokonte, pepper, salt and palm oil.
3. Wrap in plantain leaves and boil $1\frac{1}{2}$ – 2 hours.
4. Serve cold.

Method II

Prepare as for Method I, but use ripe plantain meal instead of cassava meal.

91. Emo Tew

2 cig. tins rice meal	1 pint water
2 teasp. salt	

1. Boil water, take some out and keep aside.
2. Add meal and salt, stir, using banku stick, pressing against sides of pot to prevent lumps and burning.
3. Keep on cooking and stirring over gentle heat for about 20 minutes. Cook to a soft dough, adding more water if necessary.

4. Make into four or more oval shapes, using a clean calabash or plate.
5. Dish and serve with palm-nut soup or groundnut stew, or add sugar, milk and butter and serve to young children of a year or more.

92. Ekonloma

2 cig. tins rice	$1/_2$ lb. sugar
2 teasp. salt	

1. Steep rice for 5 hours. Drain off water and pound.
2. Divide the pounded rice into three parts and thoroughly boil one part.
3. Add to remaining uncooked rice, and well, using enough water to soften dough.
4. Dissolve sugar and add to the dough.
5. Make an oblong with a slight hole in middle.
6. Boil for 30–40 minutes.
7. Serve hot or cold.

93. Bankye Dokon

| ¾ lb. cassava dough | Water |

1. Put water on fire to boil.
2. Roll cassava dough into two balls with slight hole in middle and put into the boiling water.
3. Half cook it in the boiling water.
4. Remove and pound.
5. Roll into four balls with slight holes in the middle.
6. Return to boiling water and cook well.
7. Remove and pound again, adding a little of the liquid whilst pounding. Make into a firm mixture, and form into balls.
8. Serve hot with palm-nut or groundnut soup.

94. Dzidzi

| 5 cig. tins kokonte meal | A little salt (optional) |
| 5 cig. tins water | |

1. Boil water in an iron pot, add salt.
2. Add the cassava meal, stirring with banku

stick; press well against sides to prevent lumps.
3. Cook, stirring all the time to prevent burning until well cooked (about 20 minutes). If too thick, add hot water.
4. Roll into balls and serve hot with soup.

Note: *Cassava and plantain meal may be mixed together.*

95. Boiled Corn Dough (Banku)

2 cig. tins corn dough	2 pints water
$1/2$ teasp. salt	

Method I

1. Soften dough with a little of the cold water.
2. Boil the rest of the water. Take out about $1/2$ pint and keep aside.
3. Gently drop dough into the boiling water, stir with a banku stick to prevent lumps forming.
4. Add the rest of the water a little at a time, and make into a soft dough.

5. Continue to boil and stir for 30 minutes, so that the starch is thoroughly cooked.
6. Form banku into an oval shape in a calabash or bowl.
7. Serve hot or cold with soup or stew.

Method II

1. Mix dough with water to a smooth paste; add salt.
2. Pour into a pot and cook, stirring all the time.
3. Add more hot water if a softer dough is required.
4. Cook for 20 minutes or until done.
5. Mould banku into an oval shape.
6. Serve hot or cold with soup or stew.

96. Kunme

2 cig. tins ablemamu	2 tablesp. palm oil
1½ pints of water	1 teasp. salt

Method I

1. Boil water and add salt.
2. Add corn dough, stir all the time with banku stick and press hard against sides of pan to prevent lumps forming.
3. Cook for 30 minute, continue to stir, and add a little hot water if mixture becomes too thick.
4. Shape in bowl and dress with palm oil.
5. Serve hot with spinach stew or okro soup.

Method II

Omit palm oil. Shape into balls and pour okro soup or palm-nut soup round them.

97. Boiled Sweet Kenkey

1. Prepare as for Steamed Sweet Kenkey or emo dokon.
   (Recipe ...). Omit sugar.
2. Wrap and boil steadily for 2 hours.

98. Fomfom

Prepare as for cassava kenkey (Recipe 33).

99. Boiled Groundnuts

2 cig. tins groundnuts (shelled) or cig. tins fresh groundnuts in pots	1 to 2 teasp. salt Water

1. If dried, wash and soak groundnuts overnight: do not soak if fresh.
2. Put in boiling salted water and boil steadily for 4–6 hours or until nuts are soft.
3. Drain off water and serve with boiled cassava and boiled corn.

100. Ebrow Na Kube

2 cig. tins dry corn	Water
1 coconut	Salt to taste

1. Pick, wash and soak corn overnight.
2. Wash again, add salt and boil until soft.
3. Break coconut, wash and slice.

4. Serve corn hot or cold with prepared coconut.

Note: *Sugar and milk may be added.*

101. Abrow Ne Nkate

Method I

Prepare as for previous recipe, using 1 cig. tin roasted groundnuts instead of coconut.

Method II

| 8 Fresh corn cobs | $^1/_2$ tin roasted groundnuts |
| Salt | |

1. Remove any shooks. Wash and boil corn in salted water tender.
2. Serve with nuts as above.

Method III

Omit roasted groundnuts and boil 1 cig. tin unroasted nuts with the corn.

102. Rice Water

1/2 cig. tin rice	Sugar to taste
2 pints water	Milk (optional)
1/2 teasp. salt	

1. Boil water; add salt.
2. Wash rice and boil till tender.
3. Sweeten with sugar if desired.
4. Add milk and serve hot or cold.

Note: *For invalids and children make thinner, and use more milk and less water.*

103. Boiled Sweet Potatoes

Sweet Potatoes	Salt	Water

Peel and wash the potatoes. Put into a saucepan with cold water and salt. Bring to the boil. Boil till tender. Strain off the water and dry potatoes over the fire.

104. Mpotompoto

4 cocoyams	1 gill palm oil

Onions, salt, pepper

Peel and cut the cocoyams into pieces. Wash and put in saucepan with water to boil. Add pepper and salt. When the pepper is cooked take out and grind together with onions and salt. Add to the cocoyams, and when tender stir and add the palm oil. Allow it to simmer for 15 minutes. — Serve hot.

105. Nsiho

| Corn | Salt | Water | Plantain leaves |

1. Pound the corn and remove the husks.
2. Pound again and wash and steep in cold water for two days.
3. Strain and pound and steep in warm water for two days.
4. Grind and leave for two days.
5. Steep the plantain leaves, divide the dough into two. Half cook one half of the dough and put the other in a basin. Add salt to the cooked dough. Mix well the cooked with the raw one and add water to soften it. Make into

balls and wrap each in leaves. Put in a pot with sufficient water to cover and cook for about three hours. When cooked take out and allow to cool in a basket.

106. Ametse (Cassava Corn Banku)

1/2 lb. cassava	Salt	2 pts. water
1/2 lb. corn dough		

Put water on the fire to boil, add salt. Mix Cassava dough and corn dough. When boiling add the dough and stir well. Stir continually till it becomes thick and is thoroughly cooked. If too thick add a little boiling water while cooking. Serve hot with soup or stew.

107. Rice With Beans

4 cups beans	4 cups palm nuts
1/2 lb. stale fish	Onions, pepper, salt

Steep and boil the beans until tender. Wash the nuts and boil together with pepper. When cooked take out the pepper and grind it. Pound the nuts;

put into a basin and add cold water and squeeze the fibres with the hands. Repeat this till the pulp is extracted. Strain into a pot. Peel and slice the onions and add to the soup. Add the stale fish, pepper and salt. Boil for about 15 minutes. Then add the beans. Serve with boiled rice.

108. Tuei and Ahai *(Liha)*

5 cups of corn	Water

Steep the corn in cold water for three days. Strain off the water and spread on a clean cloth or mat. Allow the corn to ferment for three days. Wash and pound. Grind and mix with water. Strain through a wire sieve, be careful not to let any of the husks go into the liquid. Put the liquid on the fire to boil, keep stirring in one direction. Boil for about two hours. Skin off the brown liquid and put into another pan. The liquid is the TUEI and the brown liquid is the AHAI. Allow to cool before drinking.

109. Ihu

6 very ripe plantains	4 ozs. dough
Salt	Water

Cut the plantain into pieces and boil. When tender, mash it with a wooden spoon. Mix the dough with a little water, add salt. Add to the plantain. Cook for about 15 minutes. Stir occasionally to prevent lumps.

110. Ode Ne Dew Nam

2 cupfuls corn	1 cupful groundnuts
Salt	Water

Pound the corn and remove husks. Wash and steep in cold water for one day. Remove from water and pound. Mix with water. Add salt and bring to boil. Roast nuts and grind them. Add to the other ingredients. Stir well and cook for 15 minutes. Serve hot or cold.

Soups

Note: *Rules for making soup used in this section*

1. Use everything perfectly fresh and as little fat as possible.
2. Boil gently all the time.
3. Use sufficient seasoning but not in excess.
4. Cook ingredients well.
5. Season before serving.

111. Nkatenkwan

2 pints water	1 cup of groundnut
Tomatoes	Fish or chicken
Pepper, onions	Salt

Roast and peel the groundnut and pound them till they look like melted chocolate. If chicken is used, prepare it and put it on to boil with the water, then add the ground pepper, sliced onions and washed whole tomatoes which when tender remove and grind and add again to the soup. Mix the groundnuts with a little water and stir into the soup. Allow to boil for half an hour. Add salt to taste. — Serve hot with fufu.

Note: *If fish is used instead of chicken allow the water to boil before adding.*

112. Abenkwan

Palm nuts	1 lb. fish
Tomatoes	Onions
Pepper	Salt
Okros and garden eggs (if liked)	

Wash the nuts in cold water. Put them in a pot, add cold water and pepper and boil until they become soft and crack. Prepare fish, onions and other vegetables, cover with cold water, add salt and put on the fire to simmer. Take nuts, etc. off the fire and pound in a mortar till the fibres of the nuts become loose. Take out and put into a basin. Mix with warm water and squeeze the fibres out with the hand. Repeat until the pulp is extracted from the fibres. Strain the liquid through a sieve into the soup pot. Put it on the fire and let it boil. Add onions, tomatoes, fish, garden eggs, okros and ground pepper. Allow the soup to simmer to the desired thickness. Skim off the oil from the top, if too much. — Serve with cassava, fufu or kenkey.

113. *Garden Egg Soup (Nkita)*

Fish	lb. salted beef	Salt
Garden eggs	Pepper	Mutton
Onions	Crabs or	
Tomatoes	Stale fish	

Boil the garden eggs, mutton and pepper together. When tender remove from the fire and peel the garden eggs, and remove the stalks or heads of the pepper. Grind the pepper and garden eggs each separately. Put a saucepan full of water on the fire. Add the sliced onions and the washed whole tomatoes. Remove the heads and scales from the fish and wash carefully. Wash the salted beef, boiled mutton and add to the water on the fire. Wash them carefully several times to remove all slime, and add to the other ingredients in the saucepan. When the water boils and the tomatoes become tender take them out and grind them. Clean the crabs, remove the eyes. Add the crabs. Let the whole boil for a few minutes and then add the pepper, garden eggs and tomatoes. Allow the soup to boil for 45 minutes. — Serve hot with fufu.

114. *Okro Soup*

Okro	Garden eggs	Tomatoes
Pepper	Salt	Onions
Mutton or fowl. Smoked or grilled fish		

If fish is to be used, place it in a saucepan with water, sliced onions, okros, garden eggs, salt and pepper. Peel the tomatoes and add to the soup. When the okros and garden eggs are soft remove them from pan, cool slightly. Remove the seeds and then pound into a smooth paste. Mix this paste with a little of the soup, then return it to the pan. Boil for three minutes and the soup is then ready to be served.

Note: *If meat, mutton or fowl is used, fry with onions for 3 or 4 minutes, then add to the other ingredients.*

115. Akatewa Soup

2 pints of water	2 cups of akatewa
Tomatoes	Fish or chicken
Pepper, onion	Salt

Peel and roast the akatewa, then pound and grind until they look like a thick cream. If chicken is used, prepare and put it on and boil with water, then add the ground pepper, onions and tomatoes. When the tomatoes are soft take them out and grind, then return them into the soup. Mix the akatewa with a little water and stir into the soup. Allow to boil for half an hour and add salt to taste. — Serve hot with fufu.

Note: *If fish is used instead of chicken allow the water to boil before adding the fish.*

116. Tomato Soup

| 6 large tomatoes | Onions | Pepper |
| Water | Salt | 1 Chicken |

Pluck and clean the chicken and cut into pieces. Put into saucepan with sufficient cold water to cover. Add salt and tomatoes (whole). Boil pepper separately and when tender grind and add to the soup. Boil for half an hour. — Serve with rice, fufu or kenkey.

117. Nkakra (Plain Soup)

$1/2$ lb. meat, fish or chicken	4 pints cold water
6 onions	1 teasp. salt
3 tomatoes	1 teasp. ground pepper
6 garden eggs	

1. Wash and cut meat into small pieces, add water and put on to simmer.

2. Wash garden eggs and pepper, add to meat and boil slowly until the vegetables are tender.
3. Add chopped onions, tomatoes, salt and fish.
4. Remove and grind cooked vegetables, and return to soup.
5. Allow soup to simmer until the meat is tender.
6. Serve hot with cassava, yam or plantain fufu.

118. Thickened Plain Soup

1. Prepare as for plain soup (Nkakra)
2. Thicken with slice of yam, or some yam or cassava fufu; or if fufu of yam or cocoyam has been prepared, thicken soup with the boiled liquid from the yam or cocoyam.

119. Fish Soup

$1^1/_2$ or 3 medium-sized fresh fish	2 pints water
4 tomatoes	1 cig. tin corn dough
6 onions	Seasoning

1. Prepare fish, add water and simmer.
2. When fish is nearly ready, prepare and add vegetables.
3. When soft, mash vegetables and return to the soup.
4. Make a smooth paste with the corn dough and add to the soup. Season well.
5. Serve hot with cassava fufu.

120. Nsesaawa Nkwan

6 fresh medium-sized fish	8 long peppers
6 onions	2½ pints sea water to cook

1. Clean and prepare fish. Put on to cook in sea water.
2. Chop onions and pepper finely, and add to fish.
3. Simmer gently for one hour.
4. Serve hot with kenkey or banku.

121. Dried Okro Soup

1 pint water	Onions
1 tablelsp. powdered okro	Tomatoes
Pinch of kawu (salt petre)	Seasoning
Meat — as available	

1. Wash and cut meat, tomatoes and onions.
2. Put all in the pot; add dry ingredients and water to cover.
3. Simmer for 1–1$\frac{1}{2}$ hours.
4. Serve with salem or fufu.

Note: *Dried baobab leaf and salem soups are cooked in the same way.*

122. Ntohuro

6 big snails	2 tomatoes
6 onions	Seasoning
$\frac{1}{2}$ lb. or 2 bundles cocoyam leaves	
3 medium-sized river crabs	
6 young mushrooms (Sibire)	
4 pints of water	

1. Soak leaves in salted water and wash well.
2. Put water in a pot and boil leaves.
3. Scald, kill and take out snails. Wash well, using lime in water. Add to soup and simmer snails till tender.
4. Chop onions and add with tomatoes to soup.
5. Remove and mash tomatoes, then leaves, and return to soup.
6. Prepare, wash and add mushrooms.
7. Season well and cook gently for 30–40 minutes.
8. Serve hot with fufu.

123. Palm-Nut Soup With Ripe Plantains Instead Of Tomatoes

1. Add half of an over-ripe plantain to the boiling palm nuts.
2. When cooked, pound plantain and nuts together.
3. Strain and use for soup making. *(See recipe 2).*

124. Nkatsebenkwan

> 3 garden eggs 2 cig. tins roasted groundnuts
> 1 lb. meat 2 teasp. salt
> 6 onions 3 tomatoes
> 3 crabs or snails 3 okros (optional)
> 5 cig. tins palm nuts
> 2 teasp. ground pepper
> 6 smoked medium-sized fish

1. Omitting the groundnuts, prepare as for Palm-nut soup and cook for two hours.
2. Grind groundnuts into a paste, mix smoothly with some soup and add.
3. Boil for one hour more.
4. Serve hot with fufu, banku or kenkey.

125. Ase Nkwan

Method I

> 2 cig. tins cooked beans 4 big tomatoes
> 6 medium-sized smoked fish
> Small piece salt fish

½ lb. meat	2 teasp. salt
8 onions	4 pints cold water

1. Prepare as for groundnut soup (Recipe 5).
2. Grind beans, mix with a little soup, strain and add.
3. Allow to cook gently for 15–20 minutes, and season well.
4. Serve hot with cocoyam or cassava fufu.

Method II

1½ cig. tins small dried beans or peas

3 medium-sized or 2 large tomatoes

6 local onions or 2 medium-size imported onions

(or less to taste)

2 garden eggs (or more if desired)

1 teasp. cooking oil.

Red pepper

Salt to taste   8 tumblers   ful water

1 or more large meat bones

Fish (optional)

1. Wash the beans and soak them overnight.
2. Pour away the water and rinse the beans.
3. Wash the bones thoroughly but quickly.
4. Prepare the onions and cut into small pieces.
5. Heat the oil in a soup pot. Add the beans and onions and toss them in the oil till it is absorbed.
6. Add the water and bones and heat to boiling-point.
7. Simmer the soup for $2^1/_2$–3 hours or until the beans or peas are very soft. Stir frequently.
8. When the beans are almost soft enough, remove the bones. Then wash the tomatoes, garden eggs and pepper and drop them into water. Take care not to add too many vegetables at a time and so stop the water boiling.
9. Boil them for not more than five minutes. Remove the skins and stalks as necessary and grind the vegetables. Add the vegetables to the soup immediately they are ground. Add the salt.
10. Serve hot as soon as the beans or peas are soft and completely broken up.

126. Pito Yeast Soup

> Seasoning
> Tomatoes
> Meat as available
> 4 tablesp. dried pito yeast
> Onions
> pint water

1. Wash and cut meat and tomatoes, etc.
2. Mix the yeast with the water.
3. Pour into a pot and add all ingredients.
4. Simmer for $1-1\frac{1}{2}$ hours.
5. Serve with fufu.

Note: *This soup can be thickened with dried okro or dried baobab leaves.*

Stewed Food

Stewing

Note Rules for Stewing used in this Section:

1. Use a saucepan or stew-pan with a well fitting lid.
2. Cut the meat into neat pieces of a moderate size.
3. Allow about $3/4$ pt. liquid to each lb. meat.
4. For a Brown Stew, fry the meat on both sides before stewing; this helps to retain the juices in the meat and also gives it a richer flavour.

5. Cook slowly and steadily; do not allow the stew to boil.

127. Groundnut Stew

> Tomatoes   Pepper   Salt
>
> 2 cups of groundnuts
>
> 1 fowl or 1 lb. meat, mutton or fish
>
> 1 small bunch of onions
>
> Garden eggs (if liked)
>
> Water, or stock

Roast the nut till brown and remove skins. Then pound and grind until they are wet and like melted chocolate. Prepare the fowl and cut into pieces. Boil, and add the onions and tomatoes. When the tomatoes are tender remove from soup and grind, then add together with pepper and salt. Add the groundnuts and water and allow to simmer for an hour. Serve with banku, rice, yam.

Note: *Hard boiled eggs may be added to this stew.*

128. Garden Egg Stew

Kako (Dzemela)	1 lb. dried fish
1 bottle palm oil	Onions
1/4 lb. salted beef	Garden egg
Pepper, salt	

Boil the garden eggs, kako and pigs feet. Slice the onions, grind the garden eggs and pepper, tear the kako and fish into pieces and cut the meat. Fry the onions and pepper in deep hot palm oil and add a little water. Add the fish, kako and meat. Let it boil for 10 minutes and add the garden eggs. Allow it to simmer until cooked, stirring occasionally. Serve hot with boiled cassava, yam, or rice.

129. Fish or Meat Stew

1 lb. fish or meat	1/2 lb. lard
1/2 lb. flour	1 lb. tomatoes
Pepper	Onions
Salt	1 1/2 oz. flour

If meat is used, wash it and boil it until tender. Fry in hot lard until brown. If fresh fish is used, clean them, coat with flour and fry in hot lard till golden brown. Slice the onions and tomatoes and grind pepper. Fry $1^1/_2$ oz. of flour in hot lard until brown, add the onions, tomatoes, pepper, and fry until cooked. Add about $^3/_4$ pts. water and allow to simmer for some time. Add the fried meat or fish and simmer till cooked. Add salt to taste. Serve hot with boiled rice or steamed dough.

130. Forowe

1 lb. fish	3 tomatoes or stale fish
Onions, pepper	$^1/_2$ pt. palm oil
A little flour	Salt

Prepare the fish, slice the onions and tomatoes and grind the pepper. Fry the onions, tomatoes and pepper in deep hot palm oil. When these are cooked, mix the flour with water and add to it. Let it simmer for a while, then add in the fish. Allow to simmer until cooked. Serve with boiled rice, yam or kenkey.

131. Joloff Rice

1 lb. rice	$1\frac{1}{2}$ lb. tomatoes
1 lb. meat	$\frac{1}{2}$ lb. lard
Onions	Pepper and salt

Cut the meat into pieces, wash and put to boil in a little water. Prepare the onions and tomatoes and grind the pepper. Remove the meat when tender, drain and fry in hot lard, until brown. Fry the onions, tomatoes and pepper until cooked. Add the fried meat and the water in which it was boiled. Add salt to taste and let the whole boil for some time. Wash the rice and add to the stew. Add a little water when necessary to keep the rice moist. Cook for about 50 minutes. Prepare as for Method I, but cook rice in the meat stew. Serve hot or cold.

132. Palaver Sauce

Fan (Efan) (Spinach)		
1 lb. meat	Tomatoes	Akatewa
Pepper	Onions	Salt

Bitter leaves (bowene)	
1 bottle palm oil	

Wash the efan and spinach. Wash the bitter leaves three times or four times. Put the efan, spinach and bitter leaves into the saucepan and meat. When the leaves are cooked, cut up very finely. Pound and grind the akatewa. Fry the onions, pepper, tomatoes; add stock or water. Add the meat and the akatewa mixed with a little water. Add the leaves and salt. Allow to simmer for about 30 minutes. Serve with kenkey or plantain.

133. Curry and Rice

1 lb. meat	Tomatoes	2 oz. flour
2 oz. lard	Salt	Pepper
Onions	2 cups rice	
1 pt. water or stock		
2 teasp. curry powder		

Put meat on the boil. Place lard in a pan and when hot, add onions, tomatoes and pepper and fry them. Remove from pan. Mix flour and curry powder and fry in hot fat. Then return the tomatoes and onions to the pan and add salt and water. Allow to simmer for about 10 minutes. Add the meat and some of the stock and allow to simmer for 20 minutes. Serve with rice.

134. Kyemgbuma

2 cig. tins cassava dough	3 crabs
2 teasp. peppers	1 oz. salt fish
2 teasp. salt	2 medium-sized tomatoes
4 small onions	2 pints water
1 medium-sized dried fish or $1/4$ lb. meat	

1. Clean and prepare fish or meat and crabs.
2. Put them in a soup pot, add salt and a little water.
3. Simmer for one hour, add more water, bring to boiling-point.
4. Add tomatoes and peppers and cook till soft.
5. Remove cooked tomatoes and peppers, grind them and return to soup.
6. Roll cassava dough into four balls with slight hole in middle of each, and add to soup.

7. Prepare and grind onions, and add with salt to taste.
8. Cover and simmer gently for 20–30 minutes. Serve hot or cold.

135. Mboteleba

2 oz. salt beef	1 teasp. pepper
1 oz. salt fish	1 teasp. salt
2 tomatoes	4 small onions
2 pints water	$1/_2$ lb. fish or meat
2 cig. tins corn dough	3 crabs

1. Clean and prepare fish or meat and crabs.
2. Wash and put them in the soup pot.
3. Add salt beef and simmer gently for 30 minutes.
4. Put in tomatoes and pepper, add more water if necessary.
5. Divide dough into two portions.
6. Make one portion into three or four balls with slight hole in each, and half cook them in the stock.

7. Remove and mix with raw portion; leave 1 teasp. of the raw dough aside, for thickening.
8. Roll the mixture into six balls with slight hole in each and add to stock.

136. To Prepare Fowl for Stewing or Soup

1. Kill fowl and allow to hang for about five minutes for blood to drip.
2. If possible, pluck bird while still warm. Dip in boiling water as this destroys vermin and prevents feathers from blowing about. Keep feathers covered.
3. Singe the bird, scald and remove scales from feet. Cut off toes.
4. Wash fowl using a "sponge" and a little corn dough. (Never use soap).
5. Rinse fowl thoroughly and joint it. Break the legs, twist and remove sinews, if preferred. Cut off head. Separate the chest from the body and cut it into suitable pieces. Cut and throw away the gall and the internal organs, leaving only the liver, heart, kidneys and the gizzard.

6. Slit and remove stones, etc. from the gizzard.
7. Cut and remove oil sack, and cut rest of bird into suitable pieces.
8. Wash again thoroughly and keep in a bowl ready for cooking.
9. Grind pepper, onions, tomatoes and salt. Return to the soup.
10. Mix the $1/2$ tablesp. dough with a little of the stock and add to the soup. Cover and simmer gently for two hours or until well cooked. Serve hot.

137. Fotoli

1 cig. tin corn dough	4 tomatoes
$1/2$ chicken	1 teasp. salt
6 onions	1 teasp. ground pepper
2 cig. tins palm oil	4 pints cold water

1. Pluck and prepare chicken. Cut into suitable pieces.
2. Place in cold water and boil for 10 minutes. Reduce the heat and simmer for one hour.

3. Make corn dough into small balls, and add.
4. Pour in palm oil, season well and simmer for one hour or until cooked.
5. Serve hot.

138. Aprapransa

1½ pints palm-nut liquid	A small piece of fish
1 pint water	6 onions
2 cig. tins kyekyere	2 tomatoes
½ cig. tins small beans	½ teasp. ground pepper
6 medium sized smoked herrings	

Dressing

Method I

1. Boil beans.
2. Wash and break fish into pieces, cut up onions.
3. When beans are soft, add palm-nut liquid, herrings, salt fish and onions, and boil gently for 30 minutes.
4. Prepare and add tomatoes and pepper.

5. Skim off as much oil as possible for dressing.
6. Add ablemamu to soup, stir well to prevent lumps.
7. Pile up smoothly in a bowl, and cover with dressing.
   Serve hot.

Method II

Prepare as for Method I, using palm oil instead of palm-nut liquid.

Dressing

6 onions	2 large peppers
5 tomatoes	$1/2$ teasp. salt
Palm oil to fry	

1. Grind peppers, salt and two onions together.
2. Cut remaining onions in slices, cut up tomatoes.
3. Fry all in palm oil.
4. Spread evenly on top of the dish and serve.

139. Kyim

Method I

1½ lb. fresh meat	4 tomatoes
1 teasp. ground pepper	8 onions
1½ teasp. salt	2½ pints water
1½ pints fresh blood from the slaughterhouse	

1. Prepare and cut meat into small pieces. Add water, salt and pepper, heat to boiling-point, and simmer for 2–2½ hours.
2. When meat is nearly soft wash, peel and cut up vegetables, and add them to the stew with the blood. Stir well to prevent lumps forming.
3. When soft, remove and mash onions and tomatoes, then return them to the stew.
4. Serve with fufu, kenkey or abolo.

Method II

As in *Method I* but add:

1 root ginger	1½ pints palm oil
4 cloves	

Method III

Prepared as for soup but don't boil.

> tripe (stomach)   6 onions
> 4 tomatoes $1^1/_2$ teasp. salt   1 root ginger
> 2 pints palm-nut liquid
> 1 lb. meat from goat or sheep
> 1 lb. heart, liver, kidneys,
> 1 teasp. ground pepper
> 1 pint fresh blood from goat or sheep

1. Wash tripe thoroughly and cut into small pieces. Cover with water and heat to boiling-point. Remove tripe and throw away water.
2. Add palm-nut liquid to tripe and simmer for $1/_2$ hour.
3. Clean and cut rest of meat into small pieces and add to tripe. Simmer for $1^1/_2$ hours.
4. When meat is nearly cooked, grind and add vegetables, also seasonings and blood. Stir well to prevent lumps forming.
5. Simmer for 15–20 minutes.

6. Serve hot with yam fufu, or serve hot or cold with ampesi, kenkey or banku.

140. Stuul

mutton or pork	2 tablesp. flour
12 onions	$1^1/_2$ teasp. salt
4 to 6 tomatoes	nutmeg

A chicken or 2 lb. beef,

1 teasp. ground pepper

A little white pepper or grated

2–3 tablesp. lard or cooking oil

1. Wash and cut chicken or meat into suitable pieces.
2. Sprinkle with salt. Place in a pot, cover with water, add one chopped onion and boil for 10 minutes. Reduce heat and simmer for one hour.
3. Take out meat and drain. Dip in seasoned flour and fry in hot fat till light brown. Remove meat and fry flour and rest of onions till light brown.

4. Put all ingredients including meat and stock into the pot. Add more water if necessary.
5. Simmer for $1\frac{1}{2}$ hours or until meat is tender.
6. Serve hot with rice, ampesi, kenkey or banku.

141. Fish Stew

$\frac{1}{2}$ lb. fresh fish	1 teasp. salt
1 teasp. ground pepper	1 oz. flour
4 small onions	2 tablesp. oil
2 tomatoes	$\frac{1}{2}$ pint water

1. Scale, clean and coat fish with flour.
2. Prepare and slice onions and tomatoes. Grind pepper and seeds to tomatoes.
3. Fry fish in hot oil until only light brown on both sides.
4. Remove fish and fry onions, pepper and tomatoes.
5. Add water and allow to simmer for 10 minutes.
6. Add the fried fish and salt.
7. Cover and simmer gently for 20–25 minutes, stirring occasionally.

8. Serve with boiled rice or steamed dough.

Note: *Curry powder or white pepper or nutmeg may be added to above stew as flavouring.*

142. Kare Stuul

4 tomatoes	1 tablesp. flour
2 tablesp. lard or vegetable oil	1 pint water
	5 onions
2 tablesp. curry powder	
1 lb. meat, or 6 fresh herrings	

Seasoning

1. Wash and cut meat into pieces or prepare fish.
2. Flour meat and fry until brown in the oil.
3. Fry onions, add flour and curry powder, fry until light brown. Prepare and fry tomatoes and pepper.
4. Add meat or fish, salt and water, and simmer until soft.
5. Serve with boiled rice.

143. Kotokyim

4 crabs	4 onions
3 tomatoes	$1/2$ teasp. salt
$1/2$ teasp. ground ginger	1 tablesp. butter or lard
$1/2$ teasp. ground pepper	About 1 gill water

1. Clean crabs, boil and pick out all flesh, reserve the shells.
2. Prepare and chop onions and tomatoes, fry in hot fat.
3. Add all ingredients, including crab flesh. Simmer gently for 15 minutes.
4. Clean and polish shells using some of the oil.
5. Put mixture in shells and serve hot with rice or kenkey.

144. Aboboe

2 to 3 cig. tin beans	1 teasp. salt
3 pints water	
1 teasp. ground pepper	

1. Pick, wash and soak beans for 24 hours.
2. Put into cold water and boil until soft. Mash

if preferred.
3. Add ground pepper and salt, also sugar if desired.
4. Serve hot or cold with tatale, kakro or kenkey.

145. Asedua

1½ cig. tins beans (edua)	2 tomatoes
3 dried fish	5 onions
½ pint palm oil	1 teasp. ground pepper
Small piece salt fish	1 teasp. salt
1½ pints water	

Method I

1. Pick, wash and soak beans overnight.
2. Boil beans until tender and mash.
3. Prepare and fry onions, tomatoes and salt fish in palm oil.
4. Add beans and seasoning, simmer for ½ hour, stir occasionally.
5. Serve hot with ampesi, mashed rice, plantain or tatale.

Method II

1. In place of the palm oil, use 1¹/₂ pints palm-nut liquid together with ¹/₂ pint water previously used for boiling the beans.
2. If preferred mash the beans.
3. Serve hot with boiled rice or banku.

146. Agusi Frowee

2 cig. tins agusi	3 smoked fish
8 onions	¹/₂ pint palm oil or any
4 tomatoes	vegetable oil
1 teasp. salt	About ¹/₂ pint water
1¹/₂ teasp. ground pepper	
A small piece of salt fish (optional)	

1. Grind agusi seeds to a smooth paste.
2. Prepare and break fish into small pieces.
3. Prepare and slice tomatoes and onions. Fry in oil.
4. Add fish, pepper and agusi paste, water and salt to the oil and simmer for one hour.
5. Serve hot with banku, kenkey, rice or ampesi.

147. Nkate Abom

3 cig. tins groundnut	1 teasp. ground pepper
6 smoked fish	2 teasp. salt
4 tomatoes	$1/2$ lb. meat
6 onions	3 pints cold water
6 okros	6 hard-boiled eggs
6 garden eggs	2 teasp. groundnut oil

1. Prepare and cut meat, onions and tomatoes and divide fish into small pieces. Fry in hot oil.
2. Prepare rest of vegetables and add. Pour in water and continue as for Groundnut Soup.
3. Shell eggs and put in stew which should be thick.
4. Serve hot with banku, ampesi or kenkey.

148. Abom Mako

$3/4$ cig. tin palm oil	1 teasp. salt
Small piece salt fish	1 teasp. ground pepper
5 onions	$1/2$ gill water
6 smoked fish (small ones)	4 tomatoes

1. Prepare and fry tomatoes, onions and pepper in palm oil.
2. Wash fish, remove skin and bones, break in pieces.
3. Add salt and smoked fish to fried vegetables, add water, and stew for 10 minutes.
4. Serve hot with kenkey, banku or ampesi.

Note: *Okros or garden eggs may be added, and allowed to cook for 3 minutes.*

149. Mmire Abom

4 big mushrooms (sibire)	4 tomatoes
1 tablesp. flour	About $1/_2$ pint water
5 onions	4 tablesp. oil or lard
$1/_2$ lb. meat or 4 smoked fish	Seasoning

1. Wash, skin and break mushrooms and fish into pieces.
2. Prepare and slice onions and tomatoes.
3. Dip mushrooms and meat (if used) in seasoned flour and toss in oil. Remove from oil, then fry onions, tomatoes and rest of flour.

4. Add mushrooms, fish or meat, pepper, salt and water. Stir to avoid lumps, and simmer for one hour.
5. Serve hot with kenkey, rice or ampesi.

150. Nkontomire Frowee

2 lb. or about 4 bundles	cocoyam leaves
A small piece of salt fish	1 gill palm oil
8 onions	4 tomatoes
About 1 gill water	1 teasp. salt
$1/2$ to 1 teasp. ground pepper	
3 smoked fish (size of herrings)	

1. Pick and wash the leaves thoroughly, boil until soft, then mash.
2. Prepare and slice tomatoes and onions. Fry in palm oil, stirring all the time.
3. Wash and divide fish into pieces and add to palm oil.
4. Add mashed leaves and seasoning and allow to simmer for about 18 minutes.
5. Serve hot with ampesi.

Vegetables

About 99% of the desired ingredients for the growth of the human body and health are found in vegetables, i.e. vitamins, minerals, etc.

They should, therefore, form a large component of your diet.

Note: *Rules for Cooking Vegetables used in this section:*

1. Soak green vegetables for about half an hour in cold water to which salt has been added.
2. Cook all vegetables in boiling salted water,

except old potatoes, sweet potatoes, yam, cassava and cocoyam.
3. Add $1/2$ teaspoon salt to every pint of boiling water.
4. Boil vegetables steadily, those with dense fibres cook rapidly.
5. Cook green vegetables without a lid on the pan, remove scum.
6. Cook root vegetables with lid on the pan.
7. Add a pinch of bicarbonate of soda to the water in which green vegetable are cooked.

151. Spinach

Spinach	Seasoning
$1/2$ oz. butter	Salt and pepper

Remove the stalk, and wash the spinach thoroughly. Boil in sufficient boiling water to cover. Add a pinch of bicarbonate soda. Cook till tender. Drain well and chop finely. Put a little palm oil in a saucepan and melt; add the chopped spinach, season and heat. Place neatly in a dish.

152. Cocoyam Leaves (Nkontomire)

| Cocoyam leaves | $1/2$ oz. butter |
| Water | Pepper and salt |

Remove the stalk and fibre of the leaves. Soak in cold water and salt for half an hour. Wash throroughly. Put down in boiling salted water and cook till tender. Cook with lid off the pan. Drain well, chop finely and reheat with melted butter, season and serve.

153. Pawpaw

Butter	White sauce
Boilingwater	Pepper and Salt
Pawpaw (not over ripe)	

Take the skin off the pawpaw and take out all the seeds. Cut the pawpaw into pieces about two inches square. Put in a saucepan and add water and one teaspoon salt. Cook gently till tender but not mashed. Drain away water. Put in a hot dish and pour white sauce over.

154. Salads

Note: *Salads should always be made from young, sound vegetables or fruit.*

General Preparation for

(a) Green Salad
1. Wash the vegetables well in cold water (no salt).
2. Dry in a clean cloth, being careful not to crush the leaves.
3. Keep the best part of the vegetables to decorate the top of the salad.
4. If the salad is made some time before using, tear the leaves into small pieces with the fingers, but otherwise they can be cut with a sharp knife.
5. Salad dressing can be poured over or served separately.

(b) Salads made from cooked vegetables
1. The vegetables should be firm and not mashed.

2. Cut in neat pieces and arrange attractively.
3. Pour over a salad dressing and decorate with hard-boiled eggs.

(c) Fish or Meat Salad
1. Divide the meat into neat portions, removing all bone.
2. Arrange green salad and the meat or fish in layers.
3. Coat each layer of meat or fish with a thick salad dressing.

(d) Fruit Salad
1. Cut the fruits into neat slices.
2. Remove any tough skins and stones.
3. Keep the best coloured and shaped pieces of fruit to decorate the top of the salad.
4. Fruit salad should be made an hour or two before serving.

155. Green Salad *(Fan, Yevugboma)*

| Efan leaves | 3 tomatoes | 2 eggs |

Salt	Mayonnaise sauce
2 small onions or leeks	

Wash the fan leaves and put in cold water. Add $1/2$ teasp. salt. Allow to stand for 20 minutes. Put the tomatoes into boiling water for three minutes, then remove the skins and slice the tomatoes. Boil the eggs until quite hard. Plunge them into cold water and remove the shells and cut slices. Dry the fan leaves by shaking in a cloth. Arrange leaves round a bowl. Add slices of onions. Decorate the top with slices of egg and tomatoes. Add dressing just before serving.

156. Fruit Salad

Pineapple (ripe)	Pawpaw (not quite ripe)
Oranges	Bananas
Sugar	Water, Milk or syrup

Peel and cut the pineapple into slices. Add water and boil for five minutes. Peel and cut the pawpaw into required shapes and add. Boil till the pawpaw is tender. Remove from the fire and allow to cool.

Peel and slice the bananas and oranges. Arrange the fruit in alternate layers in a glass dish. Pour syrup over or add milk when serving.

157. Marmalade

12 oranges	1 lime or lemon
3 lbs. sugar	4 pts. water

Wash and wipe the oranges and lemon. Cut into quarters and remove pips. Cover the pips with cold water. Cut the oranges into very thin strips. Add the water and allow to stand for 12 hours. Boil till tender. Put through a sieve keeping back the greater part of the rind. Boil pips for five minutes. Measure pulp and add 1 lb. sugar to each pint. Add the water from the pips. Boil rapidly 30–40 minutes. Test by putting little on a saucer, and when cool, the marmalade should set.

158. Chicken And Pineapple Salad

1 can (11 oz.) pineaple pieces, 1 tablespoon salad oil, 1 tablespoon lemon juice, $1/_4$ teaspoon grated lemon

rind, $1/4$ teaspoon salt, about $3/4$ lb. cooked chicken, 1 teaspoon chopped green pepper, lettuce, cress.

Drain canned pineapple and keep juice. Make dressing by mixing salad oil, lemon juice, grated lemon rind, salt and two tablespoons pineapple juice together in large bowl until well blended. Cut chicken in half inch slices, and add to dressing. Add pineapple pieces. Cover, and if possible, set aside in cool place for an hour. Add pepper just before serving. Arrange washed and drained lettuce round edge of dish, pile chicken mixture in centre and cress on top.

Menus

On the following page are listed some suggested menus, including several of the recipes listed in this book and embracing dishes for people living in various parts of Ghana.

(With courtesy of Domestic Science Division, Ministry of Education).

	Breakfast	Mid-day	Afternoon	Evening
Sunday	Sifted corn porridge or unsifted corn porridge	Kokonte (cassava flour) and groundnut	Fresh raw fruit	Kenkey and garden egg stew
Monday	Roasted corn dough porridge with palm and beans (Aprapransa)	Boiled cassava and stew. (Nkontomire)	Fresh raw fruit	Banku (corn) and plain soup
Tuesday	Boiled corn and beans	Rice and okro soup	Fresh raw fruit	Plantain fufu and palm nut soup
Wednesday	Tuubaani or steamed beans with gravy	Fufu with nerri and dried okro soup	Any fruit that may be in season or raw fresh tomato	Jollof sa em
Thursday	Maize koko (pap) or porridge	Sa em (pap) with bra soup (groundnut added)	—do—	Fufu and bean-leaves soup
Friday	Cooked millet and milk (fresh) den eggs	Boiled beans and flour with meat with gar-	—do—	Fried yams and eggs or fish
Monday	Rice and beans	Boiled cassava and palm nut soup	Fresh raw fruit	Banku and okro soup (corn)
Tuesday	Roasted corn meal porridge	Kenkey and bean stew	Fresh raw fruit	Plantain fufu and garden egg soup (or palm soup)
Wednesday	Sifted corn meal porridge or unsifted corn porridge	Kokonte (cassava flour) and groundnut soup	Fresh raw fruit	Aboloo (corn) and fried fish
Thursday	Sifted corn porridge Mpampa	Boiled cassava and bean (or ogusi soup)	Fresh raw fruit	Banku (corn) and plain soup
Friday	Boiled corn and beans	Pounded kenkey (corn) and palm nut soup	Fresh raw fruit	Plantain, yam or cassava fufu and garden egg soup
Sunday	yam or water-yam porridge (Mpotompoto)	Kenkey (corn) and bean stew	Fresh raw fruit	Boiled cassava dough and and okro soup

Sweets

159. Konkada

2 Coconuts	$1/_2$ lb. sugar	3 limes
3 pt. water	1 cupful of rice or tapioca	

Grate the coconut and mix with a cupful of warm water. Squeeze it, strain and put the water aside to be used last of all. Mix the coconut again with two cups of warm water and strain. Mix the coconut again with three cupfuls of warm water and strain. Add sugar and lime-juice to the coconut milk and bring to the boil. Add the rice and let it boil for 20 minutes stirring occasionally. Then add the first cupful of milk and let it boil for 20 minutes. Let it simmer for five minutes and serve hot or cold.

160. Pap

| 1 lb. corn dough | Water | 4 ozs. sugar |

Put the water on to boil. Blend and sieve the dough and add to the boiling water. Keep stirring until cooked (about 10 minutes). Add sugar. May be served hot or cold.

161. Atadwe Milkye

| 8 ozs. tiger-nuts | 2 ozs. sugar |
| 2 ozs. rice | 2 pts. water |

Wash and pound the tiger-nuts in a wooden mortar. Grind the rice. Mix water with tiger-nuts and strain. Put aside to be used last of all. Mix again and strain. Mix a third time and strain it, then blend the rice into the third milk. Add the second milk and put on the fire. Stir with a wooden spoon for about 10 minutes. Pour in the first milk and stir until well cooked.

162. Rich Atadwe Milkye

4 cups of tiger-nuts	3 ozs. sugar
½ cupful rice	3 pts. water

Pound and grind the tiger-nuts and then grind the rice and add to the tiger-nuts. Blend it with a little water, squeeze and strain and put liquid aside to be used last. Mix it again with the rest of the water, squeeze and strain again.

163. Rich Atwemo

10 ozs. flour	5 ozs. sugar	2 ozs. butter
2 eggs	1 teasp. baking	Milk
Nutmeg	powder	

Beat the sugar and butter together to a cream. Add the beaten egg. Sieve in the flour, baking powder, nutmeg and add a little milk if required. Mix well and turn on to a flouredboard and knead.

Then roll out and cut into pieces and make into nice shapes. Fry in deep hot oil or lard till brown.

164. Bofrot

2 lbs. flour	12 ozs. sugar	2 eggs
4 ozs. currants	1 teasp. baking	Nutmeg
powder	1 gill palm wine	
Pinch of salt	1/2 pt. warm water	

Strain the palm-wine into a basin and add the warm water in which the sugar has been melted. Beat the eggs and add. Sieve the flour and add it gradually. Grate the nutmeg and add. Add salt and baking powder. Leave the dough to rise for at least two hours. If currant are used, add them then to the dough. Take about one tablespoonful at a time and fry in deep hot fat or oil until a golden brown. Dredge with sugar.

Note: *Unsweetened milk may be used instead of palm-wine. To half a pint of milk, add the juice to two limes and beat well.*

165. Banfo Bese

> 1 lb. corn dough,   Water   ½ lb. sugar
> Lard , nutmeg

Mix dough with a little water and add sugar and grate nutmeg. Mix well. Make into balls and fry in hot lard.

166. Coconut Ice

> 1 lb. sugar   1 gill water   3 ozs. coconut
> 1 oz. butter   Cochineal

Put the sugar and water on to boil, stir until sugar is dissolved. Boil till it forms a soft ball when dropped into cold water. Take from the fire, add butter and stir. Add coconut and stir till it thickens. Pour half into a greased tin. Add a few drop of cochineal to the remainder and pour on top. Allow it to get cold. Then remove from the tin and cut into neat pieces.

167. Coconut Toffee

| 1 lb. sugar | 1 lime | Water |
| 2 very ripe coconuts | | |

Prepare the coconuts and cut very fine. Put into a saucepan and add the sugar and about four tablespoonfuls of water. Bring to the boil and add the lime-juice. Cook until brown, stirring all the time. Turn out and divide into pieces and allow to cool.

168. Groundnut Toffee

| 1 lb. groundnuts | 1/2 lb. sugar | Water |

Roast the groundnuts and clean them. Put the sugar into a saucepan with the water and fry until brown. Then add the prepared groundnuts and stir until cooked. Divide at once into pieces.

169. Alewa

| 1 lb. sugar | 1 gill water | Peppermint |

Put the sugar into an aluminium pan. Add sufficient water to cover, and oil until light brown. Pour on to a greased tin. Allow it to cool slightly and then take it up in the hands and pull it over clean nail or stick in the wall. Add a few drops of peppermint and pull until it is quite. Roll into small rounds or pull and double it and then twist it. The length should be about four inches.

170. Apofo Annto

| Onions | Herrings | Pepper and salt |

Prepare the fish. Grind the pepper and some of the onions together and salt. Have about a pint of clean water on boiling. Add the ground pepper. Cut the remainder of the onions in slices and add.

Allow to boil and then add the fish. Simmer for 30 minutes.

Note: Do not stir while on the fire or you will break the fish. Apofo Annto is good for invalids if cooked without adding the fish. Rich apofo annto is made by adding beef, sliced garden eggs and tomatoes.

171. Mfrengya

Onions Salt Pepper Vinegar

Grind the pepper and onions together. Put into a basin and add salt and vinegar. Mix well and put into a jar. Serve with fried fish, etc.

172. Garri Pudding

1 egg	$^1/_2$ pt. milk
2 tablesp. Garri	Nutmeg 1 tablesp. Sugar

Wash the garri and put into a saucepan. Add the milk and boil for 20 minutes stirring occasionally. Add sugar, allow to cool a little and stir in the beaten egg and nutmeg. Pour into a greased pie dish and bake for about $^1/_2$ an hour. Serve with milk or jam sauce.

173. Rice Mould

1 cupful rice	$^1/_2$ pt. milk
2 ozs. sugar	$^1/_2$ pt. water

Grind the rice on a stone until it is like cream. Put the milk and water on to boil. Mix the rice with a little water. Strain and add to the boiling milk, add sugar and flavouring. Boil for 10 minutes. Pour into a wet mould. When cold, turn on to a dish and serve with milk.

174. Kyekyere

1 oz. sugar

$1/_2$ pt. water $1/_2$ pt. milk

2 teasp. cornflour or ground rice

2 ozs. Kyekyere (Corn roasted and ground)

Put the kyekyere into a basin, add the cornflour, and mix with a little of the milk. Put the remainder of the milk and water on to boil. When boiling draw to the side of the fire and add the sugar and nutmeg. Add the kyekyere and cornflour. Boil for 10 minutes stirring continually. Pour into a wet mould. Allow to cool, then turn on to a glass dish and serve with marmalade sauce.

Note: *If rice is used instead of cornflour, grind it on a stone before mixing with the kyekyere.*

175. Pineapple Fritters

1 pineapple	4 ozs. flour
1 oz. butter	1 egg
Sugar	1 teasp. baking powder

Peel the pineapple and cut into slices. Make the batter as follows: Sieve the flour and baking powder into a basin. Add the yolk of the egg, melted butter and one gill of warm water. Beat the batter well. Whisk the white of the egg to a stiff froth and fold into the mixture. Dip a slice of the pineapple in the batter and drop into hot fat. Cook until a golden brown and dredge with sugar before serving.

176. Pawpaw Fritters

1 Pawpaw	Sugar
4 ozs. flour	1 egg
Batter: 1 oz. butter or margarine	1 teasp. baking powder
	Water

Peel the pawpaw and remove seeds. Cut pawpaw into slices about two inches long. Make the batter and dip a slice of the pawpaw in it. Drop into hot fat. Cook until a golden brown. Dredge with sugar before serving.

Note: *Banana fritter, etc., may be made in the same way.*

177. Tapioca (*Cassava*)

1. Wash and peel the cassava.
2. Grate it into a basin.
3. Cover with water and mix well.
4. Strain it through a piece of sackcloth.
5. Allow the water to stand for some time and the starch grains sink to the bottom.
6. Strain off the water and wash the starch several times.
7. Cover a zinc sheet with a clean cloth and spread the tapioca. Allow it to remain in the sun until fairly dry.
8. Put into a native pot and roast it over a slow fire. Stir occasionally until quite dry.

178. Garri *(Cassava)*

Peel, wash and grate the cassava. Put the grated cassava into a bag. Squeeze firmly to let out the water and starch. Cross an enamel basin or a bucket with a stick and on this put the bag of grated cassava. Place a heavy stone on it and leave for about three days to dry thoroughly. Take the cassava from the bag and spread it out to dry. When dry, sieve it into a basin. Heat the roasting pot and when very hot sprinkle in the cassava, keep stirring all the time till cooked. Then put out in the sun for an hour.

179. Cocoa Butter *(From Raw Cocoa Beans)*

1. Roast the beans in a pan over a slow fire until the shell can easily be removed. Care should be taken to avoid burning or the flavour will be destroyed.
2. Remove shell while still hot.
3. Pound up the hot beans in a mortar.
4. Grind the crushed beans on a stone to a creamy paste.

5. Then boil the paste in ample water for two hours. Allow to cool.
6. Next day remove the oil or fat and boil up again.
7. Put into a jar and allow to cool.

180. Mango Jelly

Mangoes (not ripe)	Sugar	Water

Wash the mangoes and peel. Cut and put into a saucepan with sufficient water to cover. Boil for about 35 minutes or till quite soft, pour the pulp into a muslin bag or the sieve and allow to drip. Allow 1 lb. sugar to each pint liquid. Put into a saucepan and bring to the boil. Boil quickly till jelly sets when cool.

181. Chocolate

Cocoa Beans	Sugar

1. Roast the beans till they crack.
2. Remove shell while still hot.
3. Pound up the hot beans in a mortar.

4. Add to the crushed beans half of the quantity of sugar and grind to a creamy paste.
5. Pour into a greased tin (about half an inch in thickness).
6. Allow to stand cut into shapes.

182. How To Make Kyekyere

Corn	Sugar

Roast the corn until nicely browned. Pound and grind the corn, then sieve and put into jars. Kyekyere may be eaten with palm nut soup or sugar may be added when grinding and it is used as a sweet dish.

183. Starch Kpono

2 coconuts	4 cupfuls starch
2 ozs. sugar	1 egg

Grate the coconuts and mix with water and strain. Add the liquid to the egg and sugar. Add the starch gradually until the mixture is stiff. Cut into round shapes and bake in a quick oven.

184. Dzemkple

Stale fish	Flour from roasted corn
Tomatoes	1 bottle palm oil
Pepper, salt	Onions
Water	Crabs

Boil the crabs and add salt when nearly cooked. Remove the crabs. Slice the onions and tomatoes and add to the water together with the stale fish and pepper. When cooked add the palm oil and stir in the flour until stiff like steamed dough. Cook. Serve cold and decorate top with the crabs.

185. Buni

12 ozs. grated coconut	4 ozs. sugar
8 eggs	Nutmeg Cassava

Put the grated coconut and cassava into a basin. Add the beaten egg and nutmeg. Mix well. Make into fancy shapes and bake in a moderate oven.

Note: *If the mixture does not adhere, add a little flour.*

186. Tapioca/Coconut Pap

1 coconut	1½ pints water
4 tablesp. tapioca	A pinch of salt
3 cloves	Sugar (according to taste)

Method I

1. Wash and soak tapioca.
2. Grate the coconut, mix with water and strain several times through muslin.
3. Boil this coconut milk. Add the cloves, salt and tapioca, stirring all the time.
4. Allow to boil gently until well cooked; take out cloves.
5. Serve hot with sugar.

Method II

Prepare as for Method I, but add the grated coconut fresh either raw or slightly roasted.

187. Rich Atadwe Milkye

Prepare the coconuts as for Atadwe Milkye but omit hard-boiled eggs and add one tablesp. cocoa or drinking chocolate with the rice. Increase the quantity of sugar.

188. Kokoo Mpampa *(Plantain Porridge)*

A pinch of salt $1/_2$ pint water
$1^1/_2$ pints liquid from boiled ripe
6 tablesp. fresh or sour corn dough or roasted corn meal plantain

1. Mix corn dough with water and strain (if liked).
2. Add liquid to mixture. Put on fire and boil, stirring all the time.
3. Add salt and continue to boil to the required thickness.
4. Serve hot. (No sugar is required).

189. Meat Porridge

1 cig. tin maize flour $1^1/_2$ pints of water
Meat

1. Wash and cut the meat into small pieces.
2. Put it in the water, season and simmer on a

lower fire until it is nearly cooked. (45–60 minutes).
3. Make a pouring mixture with the flour and a little cold water and stir it into the soup.
4. Continue to simmer until thoroughly cooked. Serve hot with butter.

190. Thick Porridge

3 cig. tins maize flour	2 pints boiling water

1. Sieve flour.
2. Make a pouring paste with $1/2$ cig. tin of flour, and gradually stir it into the boiling point.
3. Re-heat to boiling point.
4. Gradually sprinkle the remainder of the flour into the boiling porridge, stirring all the time.
5. Stir until the flour is well mixed and thoroughly cooked.
6. Serve very hot with any thick soup.

191. Bean Porridge

$1^{1}/_{2}$ cig. tins ground beans	$1^{1}/_{2}$ pints water

½ cig. tin maize or millet

Make as for Meat porridge.

192. Obrako

| 2–3 cig. tins corn | 12–24 lumps of sugar |
| 4 pints boiling water | according to taste |

1. Husk corn by pounding.
2. Pound again.
3. Soak for 12 hours, and pour off water.
4. Boil fresh water and salt.
5. Add corn and boil for two hours, or until cooked. Stir occasionally.
6. Add sugar and serve.

Note: *Milk may be added.*

193. Agbelimokple

| ½ lb. cassava dough | About 1 pint water |
| A pinch of salt | |

1. Boil the water, add salt.

2. Add the dough to boiling water.
3. Pour out and keep aside a little of the water, and stir dough well.
4. Stir continually till it becomes thick and is thoroughly cooked. If the dough is too stiff, add a little of the boiled water kept for this purpose.
5. Remove and roll the mixture into an oblong shape.
6. Serve hot or cold with stew or soup.

194. Rich Atadwe Milkye

3 cig. tins tiger-nut	6 lump sugar (optional)
1 tablesp. rice	6 hard-boiled eggs
$2\frac{1}{2}$ pints cold water	A pinch of salt

1. Put tiger-nuts into a bowl of water, reject any which float on top, as they spoil the flavour.
2. Wash nuts and rice.
3. Beat nut well in a mortar.
4. Mix well with water and strain through muslin.
5. Mix again water and strain.

6. Pound and sieve rice, or grind till smooth.
7. Add rice to nut water and boil, stirring all the time.
8. Add sugar if liked.
9. Pour into basin and allow to cool.
10. Serve with boiled egg.

195. Pino

1 cig. tin garri	$1/2$ teasp. salt
1 tomato	1 gill boiling water

1. Mix garri with salt.
2. Pour a little water in a plate; sprinkle on a little of the garri. Do this alternately till all garri is used up.
3. Wash and grind raw tomatoes; add to garri.
4. Serve with soup or fried pork or bean stew.

196. Adayi

2 cig. tins garri	1 teasp. salt
1 cig. tin dried beans	$1^1/_2$ gill coconut oil
About $1/2$ pint boiling water	

1. Soak beans overnight.
2. Pour off water and dry beans in the sun.
3. Grind the beans and remove the skins.
4. Cook well in the boiling water till soft; add salt.
5. Damp garri and add heated oil.
6. Serve hot with beans.

197. Bobo

1 cig. tin dried brown beans	8 onions
2 cig. tins garri	¹/₂ teasp. pepper
1¹/₂ gills palm oil or coconut oil	1 teasp. salt
4 big tomatoes	
¹/₂ lb. pork (optional)	

1. Pick, wash and soak beans overnight.
2. Boil until soft.
3. Prepare and cut pork into fairly small pieces.
4. Heat oil and fry pork slowly but thoroughly. Add sliced tomatoes and onions. Fry till light brown and add beans and seasoning.
5. Damp garri and stir it into the meat mixture.
6. Serve hot.

198. Asebetu

> 1 cig. tin peas
> 1 cig. tin roasted corn meal
> 1 gill palm oil
> 2 onions (boiled if liked)
> 1 teasp. salt
> $1/2$ teasp. ground pepper
> Dried snails (optional)

1. Wash and soak peas overnight.
2. Boil together with snails till tender.
3. Mash peas. Add meal, salt, pepper and finely chopped onions and snails.
4. Add palm oil, heat for five minutes and serve hot.

199. Akasa

Method I

> 4 tablesp. corn dough
> 4–6 lumps sugar
> $1^{1}/_{2}$ pints water
> $1/4$ teasp. salt
> A little milk (optional)

1. Mix dough with two-thirds of the water.
2. Strain through a sieve; stand until the starchy part settles.

3. Pour off half the water and put on to boil.
4. Put the dough into the boiling water, stirring all the time.
5. Add salt and boil for 15–20 minute.
6. Add sugar.
7. Serve hot.

Method II

1. Prepare as method I.
2. Roast and skin a few groundnuts; sprinkle them in cooked porridge (pap).
3. Serve hot.

Note: *Not suitable for very young children.*

200. Pomponsu

Method III

Mix the dough with water and cook without straining.

Note 1: *The unstrained mixture is better, because it has a higher nutritive value. The protein* *and B vitamins have been retained, also the husks act as roughage which helps to prevent constipation.*

Note 2: *Water in which kenkey or banku has been cooked is used as porridge or as a drink for invalids.*

Add sugar and milk and serve hot.

Method IV

1. Mix three-quarters of the dough with water to a smooth paste.
2. Boil for five minutes stirring all the time.
3. Add rest of dough in lumps (the size of groundnuts).
4. Continue to boil until lumps are cooked.
5. Add sugar and milk.
6. Serve hot.

Miscellaneous

201. Coconut Pie

(Enough for 3–4 people)

6 oz. short-crest pastry (i.e. using $1\frac{1}{2}$ of flour)	A pinch of salt
	$\frac{1}{2}$ pint (1 cup) milk
1–2 eggs	2–4 sugar
$\frac{1}{2}$ cup freshly grated coconut	

1. Make pastry, roll out and line a pie-dish or deep plate.
2. Prick the bottom and set on a basin of cold salted water till required.

3. Grade coconut. Boil milk. Lightly beat egg (it need not be frothy), add sugar and salt and stir in hot milk and coconut.
4. Pour filling into pastry case, bake at once in fairly hot oven (400 F.).
5. Reduce heat after first 10 minute, otherwise custard mixture will boil and curdle.
6. Cook until pastry is golden brown and mixture set — about 30–40 minutes.

Index

	page		page
Aberewa-Nnwe	10	Rich Banana cake	9
Abrow nee Nkatse	92	Baked ripe plantain	26
Abenkwan	99	Baked rice dough	27
Aboboe	129	Baked corn dough	28
Abolo	16	Baked plantain dough	30
Abom Mako	132	Baked cornmeal and plantain	31
Adayi	82	Bean porridge	80
Agbelimokple	81	Boiled corn dough	88
Akatewa soup	102	Boiled sweet kenkey	90
Akapinkyi	74	Boiled groundnuts	91
Agusi frowee	131	Boiled sweet potatoes	93
Akasa	83	Bobo	82
Akrakro	34	Boforot	147
Akpete	41	Brown gravy	52
Akla	44	Buni	79
Akoto	80		
Alewa	149	Cakes biscuits and Icing	23
American omelet	100	Cassava Yakayeke	72
Ametse	95	Chicken pancake	38
Ampesi	81	Chicken with pineapple	54
Apiti	8	Chicken and pineapple salad	141
Aprapransa	122	Chocolatae buns	20
Apofo annto	150	Chocolate cream	13
Ashanti Fowl	25	Chocolate	78
Asebetu	83	Coconut pie	86
Asedua	130	Cornmeal muffins	17
Ase nkwan	108	Cocoyam leaves	137
Atadwe milkye	145	Coconut buns	8
Baby-rissoles	39	Coconut ice	148
Bankye dokon	87	Coconut toffee	74
Bankye krakro	43		
Bacon and Egg Scramble	103		
Bafo bese	148		
Banana cake	86		

	page		page
Cocoa butter	14	Garden egg soup	100
Corn and sugar	65	Garden egg stew	114
Creamed celery	103	Garri and coconut	
Curry and rice	117	buns	18
Corn dough		Garri and	
pancakes	31	Groundnut buns	18
Corn Cake 11		Garri buns	19
		Garri ...	77
Dokon or Fantse		Garri pudding	151
kenkey	67	Garri salad	75
Dried okro soup	106	Garri jollof	77
Dzidzi ...	87	Garri kaklo	41
Dressing ...	17	General rules	
		for cake-making	20
Eburow ne nkatse	34	Green salad	139
Ebrow na kube	91	Grilled Fish and	
Egg and fish		pineapple	11
scramble		Groundnut stew	113
102		Groundnut toffee	149
Egg curry with rice	77	Garri biscuits (plain)	8
Ekonloma	86	Garri biscuits	17
Emo dokon	73		
Emo tew	85	Herrings in	
Etsew ...	64	oatmeal ...	100
Etsew Yakayeke	72	Herring casserole	101
		How to make	
Fam ...	7	kyekyere	78
Favourite curry	75		
Fish or meat stew	114	Ihu ...	97
Fish stew ...	127		
Fish soup ...	104	Jollof rice	116
Fonfom ...	91	Kare stuul 128	
Forowe ...	115	Kenan with gravy	36
Fotoli ...	121	Kokoo mpampa	80
Fowl ...	91	Konkada ...	144
Fruit salad	140	Komi ...	66
Fried vegetablees	40	Konkonte akankye	84
Fufu ...	82	Kotokyim	129
For Gravy ...	25	Kunme	89

	page
Kyekyirebetu	84
Kyemgbuma	118
Kyekyire krakro	45
Kyekyere	76
Kyim ...	124
Liver casserol	102
Little Iced orange buns ...	12
Mashed roasted cocoyam ...	96
Marmalade	141
Mango jelly	78
Mboteleba	119
Meat porridge	80
Meensa or millet cake ...	37
Mfrengya	151
Mmire abom	133
Mpotompoto	93
Moree krakro	47
Nkate abom	132
Nkatenkwan	98
Nkakra ...	103
Nkatebenkwan	108
Nkontomire frowee	134
Nsesaawa nkwan	105
Nsiho	94
Ntomo krakro	43
Ntohuro ...	106
Ntebrefua	74
Nyoma ...	83
Nkyemmire	42
Obrako ...	81
Ode ne dew nam	97

	page
Okro soup	100
Oto ...	78
Palm-nut soup with ripe plantain instead of tomatoes	107
Palaver sauce	116
Pancakes with ground rice and flour	48
Pawpaw fritters	76
Pawpaw ...	137
Pap ...	145
Pito yeast soup	111
Pineapple fritters	76
Pineapple meringue	53
Pineapple layer cake	14
Pino ...	82
Plantain kenkey	70
Polo biscuits	10
Pomponsu	84
Quick chicken and mushroom	37
Rice water	93
Rich aboodoo	16
Rich atadwe milkye	146
Rich atwemo	146
Banana cake	9
Rich baked plantain dough ...	28
Rice mould	151
Rice with beans	95
Roast stuffed chicken ...	104
Roast duck	52
Roasted plantain	97

	page		page
Roasted stuffed cocoyam	59	Sweet potato fruits	87
Roasted corn and groundnuts	57	Swiss muesli	103
Roasted cassava meal	59	Tapioca	77
Roast meat or fowl	55	Tapioca Coconut pap	79
Roasted corn and groundnut meal	56	Tetare	35
Roasted cornmeal	19	Thick porridge	80
		Thickened plain soup	104
Saasee special	38	To make gravy	52
Savoury leg of pork roast	104	Tomato and Egg toasts	102
Savoury pork chops	103	To prepare fowl for stewing or Soup	120
Sausage American	101	Tomato Soup	103
Savoury haddock	100	Tuei and Ahai	96
Shrimp special	42	Twi kenkey	80
Salads	138	Tuubaani	71
Spring lamb jardiniere	101	White kenkey	21
Starch kpono	78	Wasawasa	71
Spinach	136		
Steamed cassava dough	67		
Steamed sweet kenkey	69		
Steamed fish	63		
Steamed cornmeal	68		
Stuul	126		
Stuffing	91		
Sweet corn dough cake	46		